TRUST YOUR FEELINGS

TRUST YOUR FEELINGS

LEARNING HOW TO MAKE WISE CHOICES

NIKOLAAS SINTOBIN, SJ

Paulist Press
New York / Mahwah, NJ

Unless otherwise noted, Scripture quotations are from the New Revised Standard Version Bible: Catholic Edition, copyright © 1989, 1993 National Council of the Churches of Christ in the United States of America. Used by permission. All rights reserved worldwide.

Cover image by Sambeetarts on Pixabay.com
Cover design by Joe Gallagher
Book design by Lynn Else

Copyright © 2023 by Nikolaas Sintobin, SJ

First published as *Vertrouw op je gevoel* by KokBoekencentrum, Utrecht, Netherlands, 2021, www.kokboekencentrum.nl. This edition published by arrangement with Messenger Publications, Dublin, Ireland.

All rights reserved. No part of this publication may be reproduced, stored in a retrieval system, or transmitted in any form or by any means, electronic, mechanical, photocopying, recording, scanning, or otherwise, without either the prior written permission of the Publisher, or authorization through payment of the appropriate per-copy fee to the Copyright Clearance Center, Inc., www.copyright.com. Requests to the Publisher for permission should be addressed to the Permissions Department, Paulist Press, permissions@paulistpress.com.

Library of Congress Cataloging-in-Publication Data
Names: Sintobin, Nikolaas, author.
Title: Trust your feelings : learning how to make wise choices / Nikolaas Sintobin, SJ.
Description: Paperback. | New York / Mahwah, NJ : Paulist Press, [2023] | Summary: "This book is about discernment, how to look for clues in our innermost experience to guide behavior."—Provided by publisher.
Identifiers: LCCN 2022044807 (print) | LCCN 2022044808 (ebook) | ISBN 9780809156566 (paperback) | ISBN 9780809188178 (ebook)
Subjects: LCSH: Discernment (Christian theology) | Emotions—Religious Aspects—Christianity. | Decision making—Religious Aspects—Christianity.
Classification: LCC BV4509.5 .S555 2023 (print) | LCC BV4509.5 (ebook) | DDC 248.4—dc23/eng/20230126
LC record available at https://lccn.loc.gov/2022044807
LC ebook record available at https://lccn.loc.gov/2022044808

ISBN 978-0-8091-5656-6 (paperback)
ISBN 978-0-8091-8817-8 (e-book)

Published by Paulist Press
997 Macarthur Boulevard
Mahwah, New Jersey 07430
www.paulistpress.com

Printed and bound in the
United States of America

One of the things that the Church needs most today is discernment.

—Pope Francis, Encounter between
Pope Francis and the Jesuits of Chile
and Peru, January 16, 2018

Contents

Foreword by Jos Moons, SJ xi

Preface xv

Introduction xvii

1. The Art of Discernment 1
    First Steps 1
    The Actual Discernment 8
    Confirmation of Discernment 24

2. The Interaction of Heart, Intellect, and Will 29
    The Role of the Heart 29
    The Role of the Intellect 40
    The Role of Willpower 45
    Conclusion: The Sailing Boat 47

3. Practicing Discernment 49
    The Examen 49
    Giving Thanks—Thank you 50
    Asking for Forgiveness—Sorry 51

CONTENTS

    Looking to Tomorrow—Please 52
    The Inner Antennae 53

4. Discernment and Making Choices 54
    The Choice that Falls from Heaven 54
    Choosing on the Balance of Your Feelings 55
    Choosing on the Balance of Your Reasoning 59
    Two More Tips 62

5. Discernment and Education 63
    Each Path of Growth Is Unique 64
    The Deepest Personal Desire to Grow 64
    An Authentic Path of Growth Leads to Others 67

6. Discerning between Right and Wrong 68
    The Dynamic of Evil 68
    The Dynamic of Good 72

7. Discerning in Particular Situations 76
    When You Are in Seventh Heaven 76
    When You Are Angry 78
    When You Are Unhappy 81
    When You Are Afraid 87
    When You Are in Crisis 90
    When You Don't Feel Anything 91
    When You Have a Problem 92
    When in Doubt 94
    When There Are Tensions 96
    When You Have Disturbing Thoughts 97

Contents

8. Discernment and Christian Faith 100
   A God of Love 100

9. Community Discernment 104
   Contemplative Dialogue 105
   Accompaniment 106
   Common Review... 106

10. Discernment as a Way of Life.....................................107
    Contemplative in Action 107
    God in All Things... 108
    Active *and* Passive..110

Afterword 111

Helpful Links..113

Foreword

A Valuable Contribution to Contemporary Faith Formation

This book believes that there is a spiritual depth to our feelings. Ultimately, through those feelings God is reaching out to communicate with us, his beloved creatures. Of course, God's voice can be heard in many ways. God speaks through nature, culture, and society ("the signs of the times"), our fellow human beings, Scripture, the sacraments, the magisterium, theology, and so on. This book notes that one's interiority deserves a place on that list. "Surely the Lord is in this place—and I did not know it!" Jacob once cried out (Gen 28:16). Whoever discovers the wonderful world of the soul and makes her home in it, shall utter similar words.

Shortly after the Second Vatican Council (1962–1965), the German theologian Karl Rahner, SJ, pointed out Christianity had lost its commonly shared and, to a certain extent, obvious nature.¹ Future Christians would need another, much more personal foundation for their faith. As Rahner stated: "The Christian [*der Fromme*] of tomorrow will be a 'mystic,' one who has experienced something, or he or she will cease to be a Christian at all."² That has consequences for faith formation. According to Rahner, "It means that the usual religious education as practiced hitherto can only provide a very secondary kind of preparation for the institutional elements in religion." Instead, faith formation should promote the personal experience of God, or "mystagogy." And that is exactly what this book is doing. It teaches vocabulary to name what is going on and suggests practical wisdom to "manage" these experiences, with a calm confidence, knowing that one's experiences are spiritually grounded.

Thus, this book complements—and challenges—other approaches to faith formation. Usually, Roman Catholic faith formation focuses on concepts and ideas—faith *instruction*. One learns that the Creed consists of three parts, that there are four Gospels, what it means that Jesus Christ is both God and man, how Church organization functions, and what happened at the Second Vatican Council. Decent faith instruction also touches on the practice of faith: charity and ethics, liturgy, and prayer. Unfortunately, both the Roman Catholic Church and most other Christian churches tend to overlook and neglect spiritual formation. This book puts interiority on the agenda, and in so doing, it makes a valuable contribution to a contemporary faith formation.

---

1. Cf. Jos Moons, SJ, *The Art of Spiritual Direction: A Guide to Ignatian Practice* (Mahwah, NJ: Paulist Press, 2021), 7–16.
2. Karl Rahner, SJ, "Christian Living Today and Formerly," *Theological Investigations*, vol. 7 (London: Darton Longman & Todd, 1971), 3–24 (cf. the original German version, "Frömmigkeit früher und heute" [1966]).

Foreword

Trust Your Feelings also makes an important contribution to the rediscovery of Ignatian spirituality. As the late John O'Malley, SJ, explained in one of his many fine contributions, Ignatian spirituality as we now know it is a recent phenomenon. Rereading the Ignatian sources in the contemporary era has led to what he called "the construction of Ignatian spirituality." (Here also, the combination of *aggiornamento* and *ressourcement* has proved fruitful.) Interestingly, the current book is a typical example of what characterizes the last phase of the process of that "construction."

Together with coauthor Timothy O'Brien, O'Malley argues that it all started with the publication of the more than seventy volumes of the *Monumenta Historica*: a critical edition of documents related to the early Jesuits. From roughly the 1920s onward, scholars started to "mine" these sources in search of new insights into who the Jesuits were and what they did. Between 1950 and 1975, this led to a reimagination of, for example, Jesuit governance and Ignatian prayer. The authors conclude, "Finally, from 1975 until now is occurring a fifth phase of ongoing refinement, appropriation, implementation, and popularization that already has influenced countless numbers of people."[3]

Thus, after scholars have explored all the nuances of the Ignatian vocabulary, the task of translating details and jargon into understandable language awaits practitioners and spiritual writers. A daunting task, indeed! How does one communicate the wealth of meaning behind key terms such as *consolation* and *inner motions*? *Trust Your Feelings* shares the fruits of the rediscovery of Ignatian spirituality beyond the confines of the academia to reach out to all people of good will.

—*Jos Moons, SJ (KU Leuven, Belgium)*

---

3. John O'Malley, SJ, and Timothy O'Brien, SJ, "The Twentieth-Century Construction of Ignatian Spirituality: A Sketch," *Studies in the Spirituality of the Jesuits* 52, no. 3 (2020): 1–40.

Preface

In my youth, I studied a lot. I thought that the top ten centimeters of my body were by far the most important. When I finished my studies, I got to know a different way of life thanks to my friends. I discovered, to my great surprise, that you can find answers in your heart to questions that you can't answer with your intellect. I was introduced to this wisdom by people who had more than earned their "intellectual spurs." That helped me to see the world seriously. The fact that this wisdom was connected to the Christian faith was also a plus for me as a young Christian seeking to deepen my faith. A year later, I finished my studies. I started working at the university as a researcher and then became a lawyer. I was in the process of spreading my wings. I was enjoying my life as a young adult.

In the meantime, I continued to immerse myself in this wisdom. I learned that it was called "Ignatian spirituality." A tangible consequence of this discovery was that I now regularly sought out times of silence to listen to what was going on deep in my heart. Consequently, I became more aware of what gave me joy. Furthermore, I began to realize that by making choices, I could give this joy more space in my life. Gradually, I became convinced that my deepest *intuition* could lead me to discover what I was called to do with my life and to *discern* what was going on with my feelings.

TRUST YOUR FEELINGS

Two years after the discovery of this Ignatian spirituality, our group of friends spent a weekend at Leffe Abbey. During a moment of silence, an overwhelming thought came to me: *Nikolaas, you have experienced more and more joy over the last two years by living according to what you discover through this intuition and discernment. What if you organized your life so that you could fully dedicate yourself to it?* I interpreted this as an invitation to become a priest and a Jesuit. To ask the question was to answer it, positively.

Today, more than thirty years later, I continue to trust this intuition and discernment as reliable signposts in my life. In turn, I have shared this wisdom with countless people: parents, teachers, caregivers, priests and pastors, nuns, businesspeople, students, etcetera. For me, this way of life is closely linked to my Christian faith. Experience informs me, however, that it also enables many non-Christians to lead a better and more meaningful life. In this book, I want to share with readers the fruits of decades of personal experience, study, and training in discernment.

Introduction

This book is about discernment. To discern means to look for clues in your innermost experience in order to know what to do or what not to do. More precisely, discernment means paying attention to what is happening in the very depths of your heart. Christians believe that a careful reading of our deepest emotions can reveal what God is inviting us to do. The Bible, too, can provide valuable insights in this regard, but the language that God speaks today is that of human experience.

INTUITION

Discernment is as old as humankind. It is not at all out of the ordinary. Throughout history, many people have let themselves be guided by their intuition when they have a decision to make. Something that gives us a good feeling also comes across as reliable, and we act on it. The opposite is true for things that make us feel bad, anxious, or suspicious. Consequently, many people discern between positive and negative feelings and use them as a starting point for making decisions. Even if they are not fully aware of it, in practice many people rely on what their heart tells them. For Christians, the underlying belief is that these positive feelings, on the one hand, often say something about getting closer to God; negative feelings, on the other hand, often speak of a growing distance from God.

Experience shows, however, that these feelings are sometimes contradictory and can be confusing. It can also happen that we feel nothing at all. Or, indeed, we may realize that a negative feeling is a good sign. Conversely, the same is true for some positive feelings; they can be a bad sign.

> *Mary deliberately chooses to end a relationship that has no future. The break-up is a source of pain and makes her sad. Yet Mary knows she has done the right thing: She is thinking about her future.*

> *Tony finds it difficult to deal with tension. In the office, a conflict arises with a colleague over who should be doing what. The encounter quickly escalates. Tony proposes a solution that, in fact, is detrimental to his own interests. The colleague immediately accepts and thanks him. Tony at once feels calm again. In the evening, when he tells his wife about the incident, his feeling of calm has given way to anger.*

It is not easy to discern. You won't get there with your heart alone.

SUSPICION

Resistance to discernment is also universal. Many people are suspicious of what they feel. They believe that emotions are unreliable and too capricious. Feelings come and go. They can't be controlled. To make a choice, they prefer to be guided

Introduction

by their intelligence. That is objective, rational, and therefore more reliable, they think.

Obviously, intelligence and reason also have their place in decision-making. But what should you do if an important choice is presented and you have two equally good alternatives? In both cases, there are usually objective arguments for and against.

> *Derek and Charlotte are married. They have two young children. They receive an offer to go and work in Africa for a few years. They weigh up the advantages and disadvantages of staying or leaving. They take everything into consideration: their personal concerns, the children, the family, and so on. They can't reach a conclusion, though. There are as many arguments for as there are against each option. Since they don't want to end up drawing straws on such an important issue, Derek and Charlotte finally decide to let themselves be guided by what their hearts tell them.*

HEART, INTELLECT, AND WILL

In the search for what is truly important, heart and reason are not incompatible. Will also has its place. Discernment presupposes a subtle balance between these three human faculties.

Experience shows that not every pleasant feeling is a reliable signpost. Conversely, it turns out that unpleasant feelings can sometimes point the way to greater happiness. What do you do when you are in crisis, and you yo-yo from one feeling to another and back again? Is discernment something that is practiced only at major stages of life? Or is it something you can also do in everyday life? What do you do when you disagree with your loved ones about a particular problem, and yet you have to come to a decision? As a parent, how can you help your child to discern? Can you discern when in doubt?

This book aims to answer these questions and many more. It opens with a general overview about the practice of discernment and examines the role of the heart, the intellect, and the will. It then explains how discernment can be practiced in daily life, how it can help in making choices—in parenting and in knowing whether something is good or bad. Then ten different emotionally charged situations will be explored. Finally, the book will address the question of whether or not discernment is reserved for Christians and will briefly discuss discernment in a community setting. The book concludes with a reflection on discernment as a way of life.

IGNATIUS OF LOYOLA

Ignatius of Loyola (1491–1556), a Spanish nobleman and the founder of the Jesuits, is considered the greatest ever specialist in discernment. He had an exceptionally rich spiritual life, and he combined this with an astonishing knowledge of human psychology. In his writings, he subtly explains how to discern. Ignatius did not invent discernment. His main contribution is that he systematized it. His method of discernment has inspired countless people to this day, both Christians and non-Christians. This book, in turn, draws on his experience.

Ignatius of Loyola uses the expression *discernment of spirits*. In this book, we use the simpler expression, *discernment*.

This book is intended for a wide audience. It does not presuppose prior knowledge. It is a concrete and practical

Introduction

introduction within which the basic elements of Ignatian discernment are explained and illustrated with numerous examples. We hope, thanks to the expertise of Ignatius of Loyola, that it will help readers to understand and deepen the way in which they listen to their intuition or emotions.

1
The Art of Discernment

It is not always easy to discern. Various requirements must be satisfied before discernment can take place. There are also several steps and elements in the dynamic of discernment.

FIRST STEPS

Discernment requires preparation, both at the level of the heart and in relation to the object under discernment. Discernment is not about saying I like it, and therefore I will do it, or I don't like it, and therefore I won't do it. Ignatian discernment appeals to the subtle and complex richness of the human being. Before beginning to discern, it is good to go through the three preliminary stages described below.

TRUST YOUR FEELINGS

Forming Your Sensitivity

Discernment means allowing ourselves to be inspired by what we experience at the level of our deepest emotions. Feelings are very personal. That is why it is not unusual to look precisely there for what is best for us. Christians believe that it is in our hearts that we can hear the voice of God. It is there that we can find what he personally invites us to do. Christians believe that answering this call is the best route to a happy and meaningful life.

Feelings can be influenced

Feelings can be influenced. Think about how marketing works; advertising can successfully generate within us manufactured feelings. In the same way, friends, good or not so good, can have an impact on what we like or dislike. The same goes for the weather, our health, or the time of day. Think of the many people who are not "morning people."

Feelings can also be downright strange or problematic. Some people enjoy hurting themselves or others. Feelings can be perverted. Consider, for example, small children. They can be as sweet as angels. They can also be as harsh and cruel as devils and still find pleasure in it. You can't trust your feelings unconditionally. The heart needs to be shaped, nourished, and refined.

People find it normal that their intelligence is formed by years of study. The same is true of emotional life, which lasts a lifetime, especially if you want the heart to be a reliable guide to what is important. Not all so-called masters in this field are, however, sound and trustworthy.

The person who, from an early age, has consumed only fizzy drinks and fast food will find it difficult to appreciate more nutritious food and drink. The same applies more broadly to our way of living. Some people believe that happiness is no more than self-interest and personal comfort. They sincerely believe that joy is synonymous with the immediate satisfaction of hunger and thirst, the acquisition of money, power, and recognition. They find it difficult to realize that commitment to others, compromise, forgiveness, solidarity, patience, and restraint can produce far greater joy than a narcissistic focus on the self.

> *Caroline's mother has always instilled in her daughter the belief that outward beauty is the highest good. Every day, Caroline spends a lot of time in front of her mirror. Over the years, she has become very skilled at taking care of her appearance. She often receives compliments for how she looks, which she likes very much. But this little recurring pleasure goes hand in hand with a certain amount of inner discomfort. Caroline has learned to live with this. That's the way life is, says her mother. Now that Caroline is starting to get wrinkles and a few grey hairs, she notices that she is becoming more anxious. This feeling exhausts her. Caroline wonders how much longer she will be able to cope.*

It is desirable that we let our inner life be inspired by the enormous experience and wisdom that humanity has acquired during its long history. People have been discerning for thousands of years. We have learned many lessons as a result. It is not necessary for each new generation and each person to reinvent the wheel. Music, literature, dance, film, and other art forms can help to sharpen and deepen the sensitivity of the heart.

The master of the heart

This also applies to humanity's vast religious experience. For Christians, this means letting ourselves be inspired by

Jesus. He is the master par excellence of love and therefore of an authentic life. We need this nourishment and inspiration not just once but throughout our lives. Praying regularly and letting your daily life be animated by the example of Jesus means that your deepest and most intimate self will be opened, molded, and enriched by his gospel. The more this happens, the more a person can trust that their deepest feelings are truly being inspired by God himself. In this way, affective movements can become reliable signposts toward a fulfilling life, the life that God wishes for every human being.

Using Your Intellect to Prepare the Ground

It is important to listen to your heart, but that is not enough. Discernment is not a pretext for moving forward with your eyes closed. Discerning presupposes that the heart is well informed by the mind. We need to be sure that our feelings are based on a full and proper understanding of the situation. Therefore, it is important to prepare the question or subject that is being discerned carefully.

If, for example, a young person wishes to make a discernment about their choice of studies, it is essential that they investigate beforehand which options are suitable for them. Not just in their dreams, but in reality. This means carefully considering what they know about their abilities and preferences from previous studies and other past experiences. In this way, the young person will be better able to see what they are good at and what they are not so good at. They can also do research on the internet and talk to teachers, family members, friends, and people from different professions, etcetera. In this way, they can find out which studies are interesting and feasible for them and whether they correspond to their wishes and tastes.

The Art of Discernment

> *Stephen has had a passion for planes since he was a boy. Gradually, his desire to become a fighter pilot was confirmed. Stephen is now seventeen years old and has researched the best ways to prepare himself for such a job. Recently, he went to an amusement park with friends. At an attraction where there are big changes in pressure, he lost consciousness for a while. Medical examinations indicated a congenital problem with his balance. Stephen is very worried. He has come to learn that you must be exceptionally physically fit to fly a fighter plane. Stephen is still very enthusiastic about planes. At the same time, he notes that his desire to become a fighter pilot is beginning to fade.*

It may be that the discernment is about an issue that affects other people, an organization, a group, a community in which you are involved, and so on. In this case, it is advisable, before beginning the discernment, to check what others think about it or how the organization itself sees the issue.

> *Cécile has resolved to take on more responsibility in her parish. At the same time, she is approached to become a member of the parish council. Her immediate reaction is that this is exactly what she is looking for. Before committing herself, she makes an appointment with the chair of the council. She wants to know exactly what this commitment entails and whether it can be combined with her other activities. She also wants to discuss it beforehand with her husband and children.*

If you don't do this, you risk discerning in a vacuum.

TRUST YOUR FEELINGS

> *Nicholas is a passionate young teacher. Unexpectedly, a generous sponsor offers him the opportunity to arrange a weekend abroad for his students. Nicholas is over the moon. He feels that he should not miss this unique opportunity. Without hesitation, he accepts and starts to organize the trip. When everything is almost ready, he informs his principal. The latter immediately makes it clear to Nicholas that he has made a big mistake. Now the principal has a problem, Nicholas says, still over-enthusiastic. No, says his boss, it's you who has a problem: This trip will not take place.*

Discernment is not a form of magic. The heart cannot conjure up an answer to often complex questions out of nothing. The more we have weighed the facts, the more reliable the voice of the heart will be, because it will be better informed.

Learning to Listen to Your Heart

To discern means to go looking for answers in a heart that has already been well informed by the mind. But how do you do this? How do you read your heart? Many people have the impression that, day in and day out, not much happens in their emotional lives. Listening to your heart is something you can learn. Exercise brings results.

Looking back

You can only hear if there is sufficient silence and if you take the time to listen. Discernment requires spiritual discipline. Ignatius of Loyola advises us to regularly review the day that has just passed.[1] Looking back means paying attention

---

1. See chapter 3, "Practicing Discernment."

to those things that have provoked positive feelings such as joy, peace, trust, etcetera, or, conversely, to those things that have made us sad, agitated, upset, and so on. The more often we do this, the more we can detect small shifts in how we feel: a spark of hope or a moment of sadness. These subtle movements are often more important than the more spectacular ones. The latter occur only very rarely, whereas the small shifts occur all the time. That's why these barely perceptible feelings, even if they seem unimportant, have great significance and meaning when taken together.

> *Fred is mainly interested in what happens in his free time. After all, that is when a person can really live. Going out with friends, going to a match or a concert, visiting a new city—that's real life. According to Fred, on weekdays almost nothing worth talking about happens. In other words, a large part of his life seems to be a waste of time.*

Focusing on feelings rather than facts

When reviewing your day, it is important to focus on your feelings rather than just the facts. Indeed, if you start by looking first for the things in your day that made you happy or sad, the chances are that you will mostly go fishing in a reservoir of experiences that are already known, that you already know made you happy or sad. This is not a problem. It is also important, however, to let yourself be surprised by your feelings. They can make you notice things, events, or experiences of which you were not previously fully aware.

> *Madeleine lives in a big city. She is always busy. In the car, when shopping, or in the bathroom, she invariably listens to interesting podcasts. It's her way of not wasting time and staying up to date. One*

Sunday morning, while she is showering, her smartphone falls into the water and seems to be broken. Madeleine is forced to spend the whole day without her podcasts. It's been a long time since she's had such a calm and restful Sunday. What a joy it is to be quiet! Perhaps it would be a good idea to stop listening *to podcasts on Sundays from now on.*

THE ACTUAL DISCERNMENT

We now assume that you have a certain capacity to listen to what is going on in your heart and that you have prepared the question or subject about which you want to discern. Now the discernment itself can begin. The following four key points can help.

The Challenge of Inner Availability

Most people sincerely believe that what they feel in their heart is important. They want to listen to their heart. In practice, however, things often happen differently. Good intentions are not enough. Often there is a lack of freedom or a fear that makes people unable to hear intently.

When minds are already made up

People have a lot of meetings, often with the aim of coming to a joint decision. Sometimes, however, it feels as if the decision has already been made. There is no actual space for discernment, even if you want to. Imagine, for a moment, that the result of such a discernment is different from the usual way of doing things or from what your boss wants. Or you might want to know what your heart is telling you about choosing a new direction in your professional life. If you are a Christian, this may mean discerning what God desires for you. At the same time, you may have an urge to first tell God what is important to you. In this way, you can avoid God asking you to do something that goes against your own plan.

In other words, we can be willing to discern and listen to our heart, as long as the discernment takes us in the direction we ourselves have determined in advance. The result of the discernment is a foregone conclusion.

> *Josephine has created her own software company. She now has a solid team of excellent collaborators. There is a team meeting every Monday morning. Everyone is allowed to make proposals and brainstorm. Josephine constantly encourages her team to trust their intuition. In concrete terms, this usually means that Josephine's initiatives are quickly approved by everyone. Josephine is proud of the quality of this joint deliberation. She does not understand why she is picking up signals that her staff feel patronized. Furthermore, their enthusiasm for recent projects, even though they were agreed by everyone, is not great.*

Daring not to know

This is precisely where the problem lies. Discernment asks you to let go and to accept the fact that you do not know in advance where the discernment will lead. Discernment presupposes that you dare to let yourself be surprised by something that you do not see coming. It asks that you listen to your heart with openness and without prejudging and that you only gradually discover the direction in which it is pointing you. It means that you even dare to give up the natural urge to control and take everything into your own hands. Discernment therefore requires a fundamental attitude of inner trust and openness rather than mistrust and suspicion. For the Christian, this means trusting in the goodness and love of God—a goodness and love that you can feel and that show you the way to go. This applies also when the result is different from what you had thought or hoped for. If you want to listen to the Spirit of God, you must accept not knowing in advance the direction in which it is blowing.

> *A choir is going through a difficult period. At a meeting, problems are discussed. Different solutions are proposed, sometimes with much pressure behind them. The atmosphere quickly becomes tense. The singers decide to take a different approach. Each member will review the past years to understand better what has brought joy and satisfaction and what, on the contrary, has been difficult or unpleasant. At the next meeting, they will listen to their respective reflections. To the great surprise of the choir's leaders, a diagnosis completely different from what they had expected emerges.*

White rabbits

Complete inner freedom and availability are not of this world. It is part of who we are as human beings to get attached to anything and everything: to other people, to objects, to habits, to ideas....This is essentially normal and good. Attachments can, however, make us unfree. They can make it difficult to do what the heart wants to do. Sometimes, they are innocent little things, like a little boy saying to his friend, *Here is my toy chest. Since I like you so much, you can choose what-*

ever you want. It's for you. Only you can't take my white rabbit. It is for me. Our attachments can also be less harmless.

> *Arthur and Miriam need a new car. Together they are considering what is needed for the family and which model would be best for them. They can't come to a decision. There is one criterion that Arthur doesn't really dare to state, but which is very important to him: the new car must be bigger than the neighbors' car.*

Everyone has a collection of white rabbits in their own backyard. Small ones and sometimes bigger ones too. It's already a big thing if you can admit this to yourself. Becoming aware of this reality and, if possible, seeing it as something to address can be a big step forward. For some unfreedoms, it will be necessary to learn to live with them. Others might disappear over time. There is a good chance that new ones will emerge.

In short, inner freedom and availability are never complete. They are never fully achieved either. You must always be attentive and make sure that they are as large as possible. They enable you to hear better what is going on in your heart and thus to discern better. If you give free rein to the white rabbits, you can become the plaything of dynamics that you don't really want and that threaten to keep you trapped in your unfreedom.

Joy as a Compass

The person who has found their true place in life and does what they are meant to be doing will always experience joy in one way or another. Christians believe that humanity is made to live in joy. One of the challenges of discernment is to keep in touch with this inner joy, even if there are less pleasant feelings outside or on the surface. Indeed, experience often demonstrates that this is the case.

Attracting negative feelings

Negative feelings such as fear, anger, sadness, or hatred are more common than we prefer. They exert a particularly strong attraction. Without us necessarily wanting it, these negative emotions often grab our attention first when we recall the past or a specific experience. This reaction is neither strange nor problematic. We want to avoid, in the future, the unpleasant experiences to which they are linked.

We often think that the positive aspects of an experience do not even need to be mentioned. This is unnecessary and a waste of time—everyone knows these things already. What goes well is unremarkable. You don't have to pay any attention to it. This can lead to an unbalanced and distorted image of reality.

> *With his team of facilitators, Julian evaluates the recent summer camp of the youth group. As usual, there is too little time. Julian decides to pay attention first to the tensions between the facilitators at the beginning of the camp. Next, an angry letter from a parent is discussed. Finally, arrangements are made to avoid having to pay another fine next time because the place had not been cleaned at the end of the camp. At the end of the meeting, the team is completely discouraged. They had happy memories of the summer camp. Now they feel like they are good for nothing.*

Paying attention first to joy

Ignatius of Loyola recommends spiritual discipline here. He asks us not to give in to the lure of the negative. When you listen to what is going on in your heart, it is better to pay attention first and foremost to joy. Emotions such as joy, trust, peace, openness—no matter how modest or discreet—usually say something about where life, and therefore God, awaits us. Therefore, they deserve priority in our review. It is far more important to know where you flourish than where you wilt. It is more important to know where God is than where he is not. It is more important to know when you are standing on solid ground and have something firm to build on.

> *Margot, a single mother, is having coffee with her friend Karen. The conversation immediately turns to the children. Margot speaks about how difficult it is for her to raise her sons in the absence of their father, with all the decisions she needs to make on her own about education, schools, repairs to the house. Karen notices that the atmosphere quickly becomes heavy. She decides to interrupt her friend's monologue and ask questions about what is good in her life. Margot brightens up and enthusiastically recounts how her children are growing and blossoming. When they say goodbye, Margot is amazed by the deep gratitude for her children that she felt during the conversation. She is back on top of her game.*

More light leads to less shadow

The growing awareness of peace, openness, gratitude, hope, and other positive feelings has a particular effect. It allows you to face the dark side of your life more easily and at a deeper level. After all, the more you begin to realize that the light, which comes from God, is indeed present in your life, the less concerned you will be to put the darker side of your experience under the microscope. At your very core, you feel and realize that life is really present and that it is stronger. The deliberate choice to seek God's presence first has the paradoxical effect of enabling you to become more aware of his absence. A greater awareness of the darkness in our lives allows us gradually to bring these places of death back to life and reopen them to the light. Consequently, our preference for first noticing our joy can trigger a dynamic that leads to even more joy.

> Joe is addicted to porn. He finds it hard to admit it. His relationship with his wife and children suffers as a result. He feels a great deal of guilt and is terribly ashamed. During an emotional crisis, he confides his secret, in veiled terms, to Peter, his best friend. Peter reacts with empathy. He encourages Joe to become a member of his sports club and, a little later, to join his choir. During their regular walks, addiction is sometimes mentioned. But Peter always asks Joe about his wife, his children, and his work. Joe regains a taste for life. His self-esteem is strengthened. After some time, he confides to his friend, hesitantly, that he has become a member of a self-help group for people suffering from pornography addiction. What's more, for the first time in many years, he has asked his wife out for a romantic dinner.

Ignatius's preference for positive feelings does not mean that he wants us to sweep negative emotions under the carpet and ignore them. He asks us to examine where they come from. They can teach us something about what we should avoid or do differently. Regarding these negative emotions, there is a double danger: paying too little attention to them or, conversely, paying too much attention to them.

The Art of Discernment

The taboo against feeling bad

In our wellness culture, there is little room for negative feelings. Not feeling good about yourself is off limits. You must always be really enjoying yourself. You are not supposed to focus at all on the negative side of your experience. That is not good.

> *Barbara has been through a difficult time. She has now chosen to enjoy life. No more brooding. When she comes home from work in the evening, however, she still has painful memories. They make her lethargic. Barbara immediately has a drink and sometimes two or three. She often spends hours surfing YouTube or playing video games, sometimes until the early hours of the morning. In this way, Barbara manages to forget her problems. She finds it annoying, though, that her lethargy keeps coming back.*

The repression of unpleasant emotions is in fact a moralizing attitude that does not do justice to the complex reality of being human. Negative feelings do exist. Sadness and apathy are real. So is hatred and envy. In general, we do not like them. In themselves, however, they are neither good nor bad; they just happen to you. They often have a cause. The question of right or wrong arises only when you allow your behavior to be influenced by these negative feelings.

> *James has had dreams of hating his father for some time. As he thinks about it, he realizes that he has all sorts of negative feelings toward his ageing dad. James is upset. He doesn't want this. But he can't deny that they are there. He tries not to let this negativity influence him too much. At the same time, he*

> *tries to understand where these feelings have come from and why they are emerging now.*

The addictive effect of negative feelings

The other pitfall of negative emotions is quite the opposite. We can tend to dwell on our negative feelings or, even worse, to sink into them and sometimes even indulge them.

> *Suzanne is unhappy. Her husband died a few years ago. "It's normal for me to be sad, isn't it? How can I ever be happy again? I don't go out much anymore. Beautiful things no longer have any value to me. It would be wrong since my husband has passed away!"*

> *Michael feels that a great wrong has been done to him. The judge ruled against him in a dispute with his employer. He is angry, very angry. Every day, he replays in his mind the movie of the events. The more time passes, the angrier he feels. Too right. He feels it is his sacred duty.*

Before you know it, sadness or anger can take center stage in your life. This does not help anyone, and certainly not you. They threaten to cut you off from life and from God. Hence Ignatius's advice to work on understanding what is happening. Try to find out where the negativity comes from and what you can do about it. Then, when you have a clearer picture, try to let go of these negative feelings and reconnect with the joy.

Desiring to desire

This joy is so important that Ignatius not only encourages us to seek it actively but also to ask for it specifically in prayer. We have just seen why this insistence might be necessary. The negative feelings can seem so overpowering that even our desire for joy appears to have been buried. Here, Ignatius, a great specialist in the human soul and psychology, gives a very subtle suggestion. Perhaps you are not experiencing much desire for joy. Nevertheless, it can still be the case that you have the desire to desire it. If so, express this desire, no matter how fragile it may be. The desire to desire is also a desire. God can enter the human soul only through the door that is open, even if it is only slightly ajar. That is all you can do. If it is possible, ask insistently for this joy. The stakes are high enough.

> *Sarah was abandoned by her husband, Robert. Her world collapsed. She is very unhappy. Sarah cannot and will not imagine a life without Robert. She often talks about it with her mother, Muriel. Muriel realizes how distressed her daughter is. She acknowledges her pain and suffering. After a while, Muriel cautiously says that she believes Sarah still has a future. Sarah honestly can't imagine it. Yet this statement from her mother does her good. Her future still looks bleak. But these words evoke in Sarah a hope and desire that she is not yet ready to embrace fully but that, nevertheless, give her peace. Over the next few months, Muriel will say similar things on a regular basis. Each time, her words are a healing balm for Sarah's wounded heart.*

The final goal

Attention to positive feelings is paramount in discernment. Discernment is all about the continuous adjustment of one's sensitivity to these traces of life, however hidden and discreet they may be. Nevertheless, this search for pleasant feelings is not an end in itself. Primarily, it is not a matter of always experiencing more and more pleasure in one's life. These positive emotions, whatever form they take, are very important because they point the way to an increasingly authentic life. If this is what we are looking for, joy will be given as a bonus.

An Ongoing Process

You can discern throughout your life. This applies to the big choices as well as to the small things in everyday life. Discernment is a way of life. You never finish discerning. The art of discernment can always be refined. The quality of attention can become more finely tuned. Barely perceptible experiences of joy become sources of gratitude and energy. Small faults and failings that were previously unnoticed will be felt more acutely. Consequently, at every stage of life, you can grow in love and trust more in all that God offers, wherever and whenever he offers it. Increased vigilance means being able to avoid falling as easily as before into sometimes very subtle traps. Such growth requires regular reflection on daily experience.[2]

> *Andrew has taken the difficult step of going into a retirement home. His independence is rapidly disappearing. Nevertheless, he feels peace and even joy in his new living conditions. He says to his son, "I have been able to grow all my life and I continue to grow. Now even in letting go."*

Discernment does not guarantee uninterrupted peace

This explains why discerning in our lives does not guarantee continuous peace. The person who wishes to be

---

[2] See chapter 3, "Practicing Discernment."

inspired by the fullness of the life of Jesus will regularly come up against various issues in their own way of life. People, even good people, have the unfortunate tendency to attach themselves to things that do not really matter and can adopt practices of which they are not proud.

To the extent that discernment makes you more finely tuned, you will invariably be confronted with these imperfections and will wish to remedy them. Perhaps we discover that we are more attached to our image than we would like; that we constantly compare ourselves to others, that we regularly allow ourselves to tell little lies, or that we are very demanding toward our children or colleagues but rather lax toward ourselves.

Tackling all these issues usually goes hand in hand with a strong dose of resistance. Letting go of the habits and attachments that make you unfree can be literally gut-wrenching. It hurts. At the same time, it opens the way to becoming more authentic.

> *After a long quest, Gabriel became a Christian. This was a great turning point in his life. His friends are struck by the joy that Gabriel radiates. He can only agree. At the same time, Gabriel realizes that his life has not become any easier. Somehow, he feels more vulnerable today than previously. Before, if Gabriel experienced conflict with someone, he invariably adopted an attitude of intransigence and harshness. For some time now, these same conflicts have been troubling his conscience, often for days on end. Sometimes, they even lead him to question his own actions. Sometimes, Gabriel is surprised that he is now able to find compromises. All this goes hand in hand with more internal struggle than he would like, even if it is not visible from the outside. Even though*

it's sometimes difficult, it's clear to Gabriel that his quality of life has improved significantly.

Growing pains

Conversely, the absence of such growing pains is not necessarily a good sign. If your terms with yourself and your way of life are too good, if you never encounter any resistance, it may be that you have fallen asleep. Maybe your bar is set too low. Without realizing it, you may have slipped into mediocrity. For some, this is a choice. But life almost certainly has more to offer. You can and indeed should grow throughout life—and enjoy doing so. Day-to-day struggles are the price we pay for this growth. For the person who wants to live life to the fullest, inner struggle is the rule, not the exception. The fruits will not be long in coming.

Calling on a guide

Discernment is strictly personal. No one can do it for you because no one else has access to the deepest movements of your heart. Nevertheless, it can be beneficial if you are able to call upon a guide or a confidant from time to time during your discernment. Preferably someone experienced who listens respectfully and occasionally asks a question or offer a suggestion. It is a blessing if you can, in confidence, open your personal journey to someone who knows how to listen.

A friend can also fulfill this role, but a crucial condition is that the friendship does not prevent sufficient distance being maintained. This is a prerequisite for being truly able to listen and, when needed, to ask the right question or say something challenging.

The Art of Discernment

Learning to express yourself

Simply having the opportunity to articulate what is going on within you can help you get a clearer idea of what is going on in your soul. Putting things into words helps us to understand better what is going on. Something we know is there can remain vague and elusive until it is articulated. Writing can also be a valuable aid. For many people, becoming aware of their feelings, naming them, and deciding how to respond to them is uncharted territory.

> *Elise is a kickboxer, just like her two older brothers. Recently, somewhat reluctantly, she went to see her best friend's ballet show. Elise was completely blown away. She can't say exactly what went on inside her. In her family, people don't talk about their feelings. But it touched her very deeply. Now, when she walks past the ballet school, she always feels unsettled. Elise no longer knows what to do. Maybe she needs to change her route?*

It is not necessary, nor is it always desirable, to go too much into the detail of the facts. It is better to focus on the effect the facts are having on the movements of your heart. What emotions do they provoke and how do they develop? In this way, it becomes possible to discern very personal and even intimate matters in a safe and non-intrusive way.

> *Tim has been married to Helen for several years. At a work party, he had a one-night stand with a colleague. He didn't want to. Yet it happened. Tim is devastated. From time to time, he goes for a walk with his old uncle, whom he trusts. Tim chooses*

to talk about the incident. At the beginning of the conversation, Tim is very tense. This tension disappears, however, when he notices that his uncle is not at all interested in the juicy details. The uncle wants to know how Tim, in his inner life, is processing this event and how he can now best take things forward with Helen.

Being aware of your blind spots

Such discreet accompaniment can be particularly valuable when faced with important choices. If you are going through a difficult phase, having a companion can prevent you from diverting from the path. Companions can also draw attention to blind spots in your discernment.

Lewis is going through a difficult time with his youngest son, a teenager. Lewis feels that he is failing as a parent. He is totally discouraged. Speaking to another father, with whom he has a trusting relationship, shows Lewis that he has completely lost sight of the positive experience he has with his other children. With them, too, he has gone through difficult periods. But they've come out the other end. This perspective gives Lewis renewed courage and confidence. Apparently, he has more experience and know-how than he imagined.

Learning from the experience of others

A guide can also help you test or verify your own discernment against the discernment experience of the wider community. Before you, many generations have sought to discern similar issues. There is no need to reinvent the wheel each time.

The Art of Discernment

Dominic's relationship is going through a difficult time. It does him good to hear that this is not out of the ordinary at all and that it happens to most couples. The experience of others shows that it is worth the effort to hold on and that experiences of crisis can in fact prove to be valuable opportunities for growth.

Uncovering pitfalls

Conversation with a guide can help reveal traps and pitfalls or problems that have been over-inflated in our minds. Typically, negative thoughts tend to become bigger, more threatening, and more dangerous, especially if you keep them to yourself. You are going round and round in circles in your head, and the problem appears even more dramatic. Breaking the suffocating secrecy can sometimes be enough to calm the ever-growing fear. Sometimes it collapses like a house of cards.

> *For many years, Jeanne has been in a loving relationship with her partner. They have been through a lot together. Suddenly, Jeanne realizes that she is madly in love with her neighbor. No one knows it, not even the neighbor. At night, she can no longer sleep and throughout the day, she is bombarded by the craziest thoughts. Her whole world seems about to collapse. Jeanne finds the courage to tell a friend what is happening to her. As she talks, she feels the pressure drop. In fact, it may not be that dramatic. Anyone can fall in love. It is part of being human. There's even something funny about it. Of course, she needs to handle this attraction with care. Together with her friend, she explores different ways of dealing*

with the situation. When Jeanne comes home, she has regained confidence. She finds it almost unbelievable that she was in such a state just an hour earlier.

CONFIRMATION OF DISCERNMENT

At the end of a discernment, the question of confirmation may arise. The compass of joy, peace, trust, and enthusiasm is now pointing in a clear direction. The decision has been made. Now, the question is whether this discernment will be confirmed in the days and weeks that follow, as much within ourselves as in the world around us. In other words, is the result of the discernment the right one?

Inner Confirmation

The inner confirmation of a discernment usually means that one experiences feelings such as peace, trust, enthusiasm, and joy. This confirmation is not, however, often immediate. This is particularly true if the discernment is about a choice. Choosing allows us to move forward. It also means that, from now on, certain roads will be closed, sometimes permanently, because you have decided to give up certain options. As awareness of this grows stronger in the period after the choice, it can gnaw away at you. To choose is to give up. It is therefore not unusual to go through ups and downs in the period following such a choice. There will be not only positive emotions, but also doubts, restlessness, anxiety, and other negative feelings. The choice is put to the test. It is good and necessary to go through this.

The Art of Discernment

Inner confirmation means that these negative feelings gradually fade. It helps to give them their place and to see that enthusiasm, peace, and confidence in the rightness of the choice are strong enough to cope with the pain of mourning. You feel that you have what it takes to move forward with your choice.

> *Since his childhood, Simon has had two passions: the piano and Chinese. Now he is seventeen, the question of his choice of studies has arisen. Simon would like to combine the two, but he realizes that this is not possible. After a difficult discernment, Simon chooses Chinese. During classes and when he studies at home, he feels an enthusiasm that makes the study, although difficult, almost happen by itself. But the moment he sees a piano or even listens to music, his heart begins to bleed. Sometimes, Simon wonders whether he has betrayed his true passion. After a few months, the young man notices that he can play the piano again with joy in the evenings. Meanwhile, his study of Chinese is going like a dream.*

Things can also turn out differently.

> *Emily has discerned that her vocation is to become a nun. A few short stays in a convent have reinforced the desire she has had since childhood. Emily feels a deep peace when she is admitted to the community. After six months in the convent, it becomes clear to her that, even if she did not realize it, she also has a strong desire for children. This desire turns out to be so strong that the prospect of never having children makes her deeply unhappy. This sadness becomes*

stronger and stronger and overwhelms any joy. In consultation with the superior, Emily decides to leave the community.

External Confirmation

It's good to get inner confirmation, but sometimes it isn't enough. A human being is more than their feelings and thoughts. They are also embodied and live in a specific place and time. They exist amid a host of human relationships, whether in the family, in the church, or through professional and other commitments. These external realities form the objective world within which a person lives. A personal discernment must also be confirmed by the outside world if it is to be real and achievable. You do not discern in a vacuum.

Eugenie is getting older. She plans to move to the city. After giving the matter some thought and making inquiries, she takes the time to discern. Her discernment leads her to sell her farm and look for an apartment in town. Sometimes, Eugenie feels anxiety and sadness. At the same time, she feels that her choice to move is the right one. She is now completely confident in her decision. It turns out, however, that nobody wants to buy Eugenie's little farm. A few weeks ago, it was announced that a new highway would be built next to her farmhouse. This sad reality calls into question her choice that was so well discerned!

Brother Joseph is the charismatic founder and superior of a Christian community in a large city. Silence and prayer are at the heart of the project. Over the years, the community has grown and structures for consultation have emerged. For some time, Brother Joseph has had the feeling that the community should also make a social commitment. After a long period of personal discernment, this has been transformed into an inner certainty. He gathers the community to make his conviction known. The Rule of Life provides that major changes must be approved by at least three-quarters of the members. Brother Joseph doubts that his plan will receive sufficient support. After a few weeks, a vote takes place. This shows that the community is almost unanimously in favor of Joseph's proposal. It is now possible to make a concrete commitment in this new direction.

Confirmation by the Fruits

There is another form of external confirmation. The fruits of the choice, those things that the choice brings or produces, can also be part of the confirmation.

> Henry, Alice, and their children have chosen to move. The whole family quickly feels comfortable in the new house and the new town. Any doubts have now been dispelled.

> Emma has chosen to stop working for someone else and become self-employed instead. The market for freelance journalists, however, is not in good shape. Nevertheless, after only a few months, she has enough contracts and earns a decent living. Emma feels at home in this new professional environment, even though she doubted beforehand whether it would suit her.

Time and Patience

The question of confirmation clearly shows that time and patience are necessary for discernment. You cannot discern in haste. Discernment is not a purely technical operation that occurs at the touch of a button—although some certainly wish that was the case. Our digital culture has familiarized us with the immediate. But there is no such thing as a discernment algorithm. Discernment is a step-by-step process. Experiences, perspectives, and alternatives need time to be weighed and gauged by the heart. Listening to the Spirit of God, like any human reality, is subject to the law of slowness.

> *Quentin holds a position of responsibility in a hospital. He is passionate about his work. Nevertheless, he accepts an offer to become the manager of a large retirement home within the same group. Quentin likes it very much. His daily commute, however, is now much longer. He sometimes needs to deal with cases that take him out of his comfort zone. After a few years, his former boss asks him to return, with the bonus of a generous pay rise. Quentin doesn't immediately know what to do. Those around him are astonished by what they regard as indecision. Quentin doesn't allow himself to be distracted. He has made the choice to take his time and to discern. Once his decision has been made, he gives himself additional time to see if his choice is confirmed.*

2

The Interaction of Heart, Intellect, and Will

THE ROLE OF THE HEART

Discernment does not mean getting carried away by superficial emotions. Even less, that objective and impersonal reasoning prevails. Nor that moving forward in life is ultimately a matter of strength of will. Ignatian discernment is based on the subtle interaction of these three important human faculties: heart, intellect, and will. This chapter examines the contribution of each of these elements.

The starting point and the raw material of discernment is what happens in the heart. Listening to one's feelings is, however, more complicated than it seems.

What Feelings Are We Talking About?

Human emotions occur on different levels. Not all of them lend themselves to discernment.

Discernment does not take place at the level of the superficial or outer layers of emotional feeling. It is not a question of whether you started the day well or whether you got out on the wrong side of the bed. This would quickly lead to superficial feelings dictating your life: I like it, so I do it, or I don't like it, so I don't do it. Nor is discernment based on brief, often artificially generated emotions. Thrills can certainly produce adrenaline. They can give pleasure. In the end, they leave few lasting traces. They can also leave you with a feeling of emptiness.

> *Laura often feels lonely. Recently, she installed the dating app Tinder on her smartphone. Her friends assure Laura that it will change her life. Laura now has one-night stands from time to time. It flatters her ego. These encounters are usually nice. She also likes the excitement in the hours before the date. She likes to brag about her successes with her girlfriends. But she doesn't tell them everything. When her one-night stand leaves her in the morning, she feels miserable. Afterward, it takes her several days to regain her equilibrium.*

What's more, these superficial or artificially induced feelings can be easily manipulated. Advertising and digital technology take full advantage of them. They are unreliable when it comes to making a discernment.

The Interaction of Heart, Intellect, and Will

Emotional interiority

Discernment requires us to connect instead with the feelings that develop at a deeper level of experience: the level that is the emotional foundation or source of life, the level of our interiority. This is where you find the feelings that do not change all the time. They are much less likely to be manipulated; they last longer, do not depend on hormones or the weather, and say something about what is really important to you. They are usually not very intense, which is why they are often less easy to identify. Because of their longer duration, however, their impact and importance are great. This emotional foundation says something about the truth of your life. Interiority is the place where Christians believe they can hear the voice of God.

Positive and negative feelings in concrete terms

Positive feelings at this deepest level generally reveal the path that brings you ever closer to truly authentic living. For Christians, they are often a sign of a deepening connection with God. They can take many forms. Concretely, they can be feelings such as trust, peace, gratitude, love, joy, yearning, inner strength, energy, cheerfulness, security, a relish for life, calm, gentleness, passion, enthusiasm, motivation, connection, openness, curiosity, and contentment. You can also feel something at the level of insight and intelligence: feeling that you are getting an answer, that your mind is becoming more open, that the pieces of the puzzle are coming together, or that you finally understand what it is all about.

TRUST YOUR FEELINGS

Negative feelings generally indicate the path away from life and therefore to greater distance from God. These feelings include bitterness, sadness, harshness, withdrawal, revulsion, coldness, restlessness, irritation, discomfort, torment, frustration, distrust, fear, jealousy, cynicism, self-pity, hatred, depression, emptiness, apathy, feeling lost, dejection, and demotivation. Negative feelings can also be expressed intellectually, for example, in confusion, distraction, or experiencing difficulty in understanding.

Your own feelings

A common mistake in discernment is that people do not give due weight to their own feelings. They attach so much importance to the views of those close to them that they tend to put their own feelings in brackets. This can go so far that, instead of listening to their own heart, people let themselves be led by the feelings of others.

> *For the first time in his life, Alexander tries out a silent retreat at an abbey. The peace and quiet are a blessing in that Alexander has never come so close to the very essence of his life. It leaves him with a taste for more. But the return home is painful. His roommates are annoyed by his story. They tell him it sounds like brainwashing. Alexander hesitates: Is it a good idea to do another retreat like this? Yet he continues to feel good and deeply at peace when he reflects on the weekend.*

Of course, it is important to know what people around you think and feel about the important things in your life. Especially when it comes to people who love you and therefore really know you. From their feelings, you can draw out important information about what is or is not important to you.

The Interaction of Heart, Intellect, and Will

Moreover, to a certain extent, their life is also part of yours. So, it is good to consider what their heart tells them. But ultimately, your own heart is the only place where all the information comes together. You are the only person who can discern what is important to you.

> *Anne is married to John. She has been a high school teacher for fifteen years. Soon the school principal will retire. John thinks that his wife is the ideal candidate to replace him. This would make John proud and happy. But Anne doesn't feel that way at all. Her vocation is to teach and to be in contact with young people. The prospect of becoming a manager leaves her cold. Anne now has trouble sleeping. She loves her husband very much. She values his opinion and his feelings and asks for them. Nevertheless, she chooses to let her own feelings be the deciding factor. After all, it is Anne who will have to take responsibility for her choice.*

Your own feelings are the indispensable starting point for discernment. Of course, this does not mean that other people's feelings are irrelevant. It may well be useful to consider them, but in an appropriate way.

> *Alex loves her little brother, Sebastian, and vice versa. Sebastian is a keen basketball player. Basketball is of no interest to Alex. Nevertheless, Alex regularly goes to see Sebastian's games. She knows that he is always happy when his big sister supports him. She realizes that Sebastian would love it if she too played basketball. But after every one of his games, Alex goes running. That's her sport. She absolutely wants to keep it that way.*

TRUST YOUR FEELINGS

Aftertaste

Finally, it is also important to consider the longer-term emotional experience. Ignatius advises not to pay attention to our emotions only at the time of the experience itself. To discern properly, it is necessary to consider the aftertaste of the experience.

An event can be accompanied by great joy, but afterward it can leave you with a hangover. Or, if you think about it again later, you no longer feel any joy at all but rather sadness and emptiness.

> *Mark was furious with his colleague and made sure he knew this immediately, and in a not very subtle way. At the time of his eruption, he felt a certain release. But now he has a hard time engaging with this colleague with whom he had a good working relationship.*

Conversely, you can experience something, in the moment, as difficult and even painful. At the same time, you may find that, on a deeper level, it eventually brings you peace and happiness.

> *Lucy is a doer more than a thinker. She knows from experience that training courses can be a challenge for her. They make her feel insecure and nervous. She misses her work environment and counts the hours. Lucy also knows that she always feels satisfied after a training course. Experience has taught her that, in the end, the training does her good. Even though there are always negative feelings associated with these courses, Lucy signs up for them every year.*

The Interaction of Heart, Intellect, and Will

This positive or negative aftertaste is an important clue as to whether an attitude, relationship, experience, or event is, for you, a path to either more or less life.

Feelings versus Ideals, Values, and Customs

It is a blessing if your education has given you a solid grounding in values and social norms. These are valuable building blocks for the development of a personality. They are beacons that can help you find your way, every day, in our sometimes-crazy world. In discernment, however, it is important not to confuse your feelings with these ideals, values, and customs.

Tools, not binding directives

Ideals, values, and customs are external and fixed. As such, they say nothing about what, in a particular case, is important or meaningful to you and what is the best way for you to proceed. They are a useful resource. No less, but no more.

In concrete terms, this means that your heart can give you signals that are diametrically opposed to certain ideals, values, or customs that are important to you. This does not mean that these values or social norms should no longer be important to you. It simply means that your heart, in this concrete situation, gives priority to other values and, consequently, points in a different direction.

> *Nathan gives great weight to the idea of a fairer world. He is asked to take on, in his free time, a responsibility in a humanitarian organization. Nathan*

does not feel at all comfortable with this proposal. He notices growing restlessness and tension within himself. The proposal paralyzes Nathan, much more than giving him energy. How is it possible to feel bad about something that seems to suit him perfectly? When he starts to give it more thought, it becomes clear that he simply doesn't have the time to give. Nathan is already overcommitted. It would be a bad idea to say yes. Moderation is also important. That is the message his heart gives him.

Objective Feelings

Sometimes you hear things like:

I feel that I can never forgive my parents for this.
I feel that I have to take my child out of this school.
I feel that I need to buy a new car.

Strictly speaking, these are not about feelings. There is no specific feeling that corresponds to not being able to forgive or to changing a child's school or your car. Instead, it is about the interpretation of facts and any feelings such as anger, annoyance, or frustration that are associated with them.

This distinction between facts and feelings is important. Feelings are, by definition, personal and subjective. Every human being is affected in a unique way by events. At the same time, there is also something objective and undeniable about feelings: joy is joy; sadness is sadness; and hope is hope. There is not much discussion possible on this subject.

Not I feel that...

One pitfall is that many people immediately interpret their feelings and, as a result, capture them in analysis, resolutions, and the like. There is, however, something elusive about feelings. They are beyond our control. By trying to explain or interpret them, we put our intellect in control. It feels safe. There is nothing wrong with that. But if we allow these interpretations to be preceded by *I feel that*, then they are given an appearance of objectivity and therefore of indisputability, like real feelings. The interpreter can be wrong, however, even when it comes to the interpretation of their own feelings. Thus, from the outset, the discernment is in danger of being rooted in false assumptions. We can, with every good intention, deceive ourselves.

> *Julie takes dance classes. The reason she gave for signing up is her lack of rhythm. In fact, Julie just doesn't feel very good in her body. This is a sensitive issue for her. She hopes that dance can help her. The dance teacher soon realizes that Julie is struggling. From time to time, he discreetly suggests she rightly connect with her problem. As has happened so often, she reaches a conclusion that is in fact just running away: "I feel that this dance teacher is no good. I'd better stop the dance class." Julie could have had a conversation with the dance teacher. He might have suggested that she go and talk to a psychologist. Now, for the umpteenth time, Julie is playing hide-and-seek with herself.*

More like I feel...

If you really want to discern, it is necessary to start at the level of original, unprocessed feelings. These must then be placed next to the facts that gave rise to the feelings. With your intelligence you can then look for a possible explanation. There is a simple technique to avoid missing these raw feelings. Do not start your sentence with *I feel that* because, after these words, an interpretation almost inevitably follows. It is better to start with *I feel*. Then it is more likely that you will come directly to the feeling itself, the raw material of discernment.

> *In the dance class, Julie simply felt uncomfortable, anxious, and pressured because she was forced to deal with her body. The dance teacher gently invited her to work through her blockage. By saying "I feel that he is not a good teacher," she made this impossible. Under the pretext of taking her feelings seriously, Julie has silenced them and left herself with a false explanation.*

Feelings Can Be Ambivalent

Not all negative feelings lead in the wrong direction. Conversely, not all positive feelings point in the right direction.

Anyone who has made a serious mistake can experience intense remorse. Remorse means being sorry for what has happened and planning not to do it again in the future. Remorse is no fun. It hurts. It is an unpleasant feeling, but it is also a sign that you are on the right track.

People make fun of each other a lot. Some people find it amusing. Most people agree that picking on someone is not to be recommended. Yet, in some ways, it is accompanied by pleasant feelings. Especially in the moment.

The evil angel who turns into an angel of light

The situation can be much more subtle.

> *Ellen is a student and must hand in a paper on Monday. She needs her weekend to work. Ellen is no great*

The Interaction of Heart, Intellect, and Will

> *musician, but without knowing why, on Friday evening, for the first time in months, she takes up her guitar again. She loves it. Good idea, says a little voice in her heart. You haven't played for way too long. Ellen makes music for hours over the weekend, with passion and a sense of satisfaction. On Sunday evening, her paper is not ready. She clearly has a problem and feels rotten, yet playing her guitar felt so good.*

Ignatius uses a rather special image here. He is talking about the evil angel who turns into an angel of light. Under the appearance of something good—the angel of light—you are, in fact, being pushed in the wrong direction by darker forces. That voice encouraged Ellen to play her guitar so that she wouldn't lose the skill completely. Her feelings of pleasure and enjoyment, it seemed, confirmed that it was a good idea, didn't they? It turned out to be a trap.

Righteous anger

Anger does not normally point the way to more life and is, therefore, best avoided. But there is such a thing as righteous anger: anger that is motivated solely by indignation at injustice and that can therefore have a positive effect.

> *A well-known example is the scene in the Gospel where an angry Jesus drives out the traders and money changers from the Temple in Jerusalem. He reproaches them for turning the house of God into a den of thieves.*

Experience shows that it is better to be careful when it comes to welcoming—or not—anger when you feel it rising to the surface. Righteous anger is given to only a few people. Often, anger has more to do with personal irritation, helplessness, fatigue, or a wounded ego than with righteous indignation. What is remarkable is that listeners are often perfectly able to distinguish between this exceptional righteous anger and ordinary, purely human anger. As soon as people notice that the latter is involved, even if there is also some righteous anger, the effect is likely to be negative.

The conclusion is clear. Feelings can be ambiguous. It is necessary to interpret them. Discernment is not only with the heart. Intellect is also important.

THE ROLE OF THE INTELLECT

Ignatian discernment takes as its starting point those things that occur at the level of our foundational feelings. Emotional experience is the raw material. The intellect—objective reason—is also important, although literally secondary. In the dynamics of Ignatian discernment, it is up to our intellect to process the information provided by the heart.

Becoming Aware of Inner Feelings

The intellect can help us become more aware of what is going on in our heart. Articulating feelings can be an important step in this process.

For most people, it is not easy to listen to their feelings. Even if they are aware of their deeper emotional life, they are often suspicious of it or try to sweep the feelings it produces under the carpet. Feelings can scream loudly. But many never think to listen to them.

The Interaction of Heart, Intellect, and Will

Eva calls her best friend. She immediately starts crying. For the umpteenth time, she has had an argument with her sister. Sobbing, she tells how the quarrel started. She is very unhappy. But, as she repeats several times during the conversation, I'm right. I did the right thing. After Eva has unburdened herself and calmed down a bit, her friend says cautiously, "You say you'll do the same thing next time. But if your attitude toward your sister is really the right one, how come you are so sad?" Eva doesn't know what to say any more. She had never thought of it that way.

Listening to what's going on with your emotions at the deepest level, expressing your feelings and taking them seriously, is something you can learn. Practice makes perfect. Talking to a wise person can be helpful. But such a person is not always immediately available. The simplest tool for learning how to listen to your feelings is the previous section: Consciously take time to reflect on your experience and attentively look for what touched you and how it affected you.[1]

Interpretation of Inner Feelings

The next step is to order and interpret your feelings. Inner feelings can seem complex, contradictory, and chaotic. What first feels good can end badly and vice versa. Intelligence makes it possible to read your feelings. Sharper insights can emerge about your feelings and what they reveal about what is most important to you and how you can best respond. Christians believe that in this way they can discover God's desire for them in their hearts.

---

1. See also chapter 3, "Practicing Discernment."

TRUST YOUR FEELINGS

Different levels of feelings

Intelligence makes it possible to take some distance from the immediate experience to discern between the different levels of feelings. There is not only the upper level of feelings, which are often superficial and fleeting. Underneath lies another, deeper, and more stable level: the emotional foundation. The resources offered by the intellect can ensure that you do not get carried away by the volatility of feelings at the higher level. You can learn to stay connected with those more fundamental feelings.

> *By the end of the day, Louise is at her wits' end with this teenager who wanders around her house. She feels desperate and angry. Will it never end? For years, Louise has been in the habit of reviewing her day at the end of the evening. Tonight, too, this time of looking back allows her, despite the negativity, to regain deeper peace and trust that, she knows from experience, are also there. She knows that these unpleasant episodes occur from time to time. But she also knows that she is doing the right thing and that it makes sense for her to resist her daughter's whims. All in all, this teenage girl is doing well. A little more time and the worst will have passed.*

Common threads

The more often you review, the more aware you become of what is going on in your inner life and of possible recurring emotions. If you then regularly give yourself time to take a few notes on the fruits of your review, you will probably notice patterns emerging. Common threads or themes appear. We can see that this attitude, this activity, this event, or this relationship is connected more to positive or negative feelings.

The Interaction of Heart, Intellect, and Will

When Theo is tired or tense, he tends to withdraw into himself. He worries about anything and everything, and often painful memories of a difficult period in his life resurface. The end point is always the same: he feels deeply unhappy, which leads to tension with his partner, Hugo. But Theo has also noticed that, if he goes for an extra jog or does some work in the garden, he sleeps well afterward and is back to his usual self the next day. It is Theo's regular review of his day that has made him aware of this movement.

Thus, the objective mind, through regular reflection and review, makes it possible to learn from experience so as to avoid falling into the same traps over and over again.

The course of emotions

By paying attention to the way feelings develop, you can learn and grow in who and what you are. Discontinuity or change can be especially significant.

For example, at the beginning of an experience or an event, you can feel buoyed by confidence, hope, and energy. Everything is going well. This pleasant feeling gradually fades, however. In the end, there is anxiety, despondency, or anger. Ignatius advises us to review things carefully, working backward. The aim is to go back into your memory to the precise moment when the positive feelings turned into negative feelings. What is the cause of this reversal? What happened? Perhaps this says something about the way you deal with certain issues or the impact of specific relationships. Such insights can inspire you to change your behavior. In this way, you learn by reflecting on your life in a discerning way.

Sophie works with a medical team. She is creative and has an idea to improve the organization. She is supported by her bosses. She starts with a lot of enthusiasm. After a while she realizes that the reorganization risks going wrong. Relationships with colleagues become difficult. Management starts to have doubts. At first, Sophie felt full of energy, but now she has become anxious and hesitant. She starts to lose courage. Her review is direct and honest. She realizes that things started to go wrong as soon as she had to collaborate with her colleagues. In fact, she wanted to decide everything herself. She didn't let others have their say. She knows why. It's her lack of self-confidence that causes the problem. This awareness is liberating. Even if it is difficult for her, Sophie now consciously chooses really to involve her colleagues in the delivery of the reorganization. In the end, everything goes well. Her creative idea has led to an excellent reorganization, and Sophie has grown as a person. She has a great sense of satisfaction.

The criterion of duration

When looking back, it is useful to notice how long the feelings last. It may be that the joy you feel continues after the event that caused it. Or that the memory of an experience repeatedly fills you with joy. This usually indicates that what has happened is good for you.

Conversely, you can notice that an experience is pleasant at the time but that afterward it no longer makes you happy at all.

> *Luke regularly has a drink with Augustine after work. Luke and Augustine are good friends. Nevertheless, Luke observes that, after their weekly get-together,*

he feels increasingly empty and dissatisfied. At first, they played sports together, after which they would take time to talk quietly. But lately, they have stopped doing sports and now all they do is drink. Looking back, Luke realizes that they are gossiping more and more about colleagues during these encounters.

THE ROLE OF WILLPOWER

The will is the third and last actor in discernment, after the heart and the intellect. The will allows you to complete the discernment by making its conclusions a lived reality.

The will concerns the ability to decide, to make choices, and to stick to them. The will makes it possible to live more in accord with the yearning of your heart that you have discerned with your mind. Conversely, the will also makes it possible to avoid pitfalls. You can consciously choose not to give in to the lure of superficial joy, which you have learned can end in tears or with a hangover. In this way, you can deliberately steer your life in the direction that brings lasting joy.

For Luke, the matter is clear. He wants to consider what he has discerned about the course of his weekly meetings with Augustine. Their friendship is dear to him, but this gossip cannot continue. He decides to talk to Augustine about it at their next meeting. Augustine isn't happy with the gossip either. So, they decide to get back into sport. They both also decide to avoid gossip from now on.

The will is thus not in opposition to the heart. On the contrary, the will allows the fruits of discernment to be reaped in practice. By making choices, a person can consciously give direction to their life. The will can therefore help a person become freer, to become someone who consciously chooses according to what they deeply feel to be their calling, rather than someone who is constantly getting stuck in ruts or caught in traps.

The Impasse of Voluntarism

The will is the final element in the dynamics of a successful discernment. It comes only in third place and is subordinate to the heart and the intellect. In some people, however, the will is given first place. This is called voluntarism—a will that is detached from its real desires and that sets its own priorities. Voluntarism often leads to an impasse.

> *Chloe is a girl who likes to work with her hands, if possible, creatively and artistically. In this way she is fully herself and feels passion and strength. The results of her previous studies clearly show that the sciences do not suit her. Nevertheless, Chloe decides to study physics. She does it to please her parents. She works like crazy. Her willpower and strength of character are impressive. The results are very disappointing. After two years, Chloe is totally discouraged, not far from burnout.*

The will can make its full contribution only if it puts itself at the service of the desires that the intellect has discerned in the heart.

> *After another series of poor exam results, Chloe goes to see her tutor, who finally convinces Chloe to change her studies. She now enrolls in an applied design course. She lives again. She works just as*

hard as before. Only now it fits who she is, and she enjoys every day.

CONCLUSION: THE SAILING BOAT

Discernment is like sailing a boat on a large body of water when the wind is strong. Success depends on the wind, the sailor, and the rudder.

The direction of the wind is like the voice of the heart. It speaks a person's deepest desire. It expresses what sets them in motion and moves them forward. It is there. There is no need to invent this desire yourself. You don't choose what it looks like. It is simply given.

The sailor is like the mind. She judges the direction and strength of the wind so as to respond optimally. Her role is crucial. Without a sailor, the ship has no direction and is at risk of rapid damage. You can have the impression that the sailor could choose any direction. Not so. She must constantly take the direction of the wind into account. Without the wind, the sailor can do nothing.

The rudder, finally, is like the will. Thanks to the rudder, the direction given to the boat by the sailor becomes real. It gives the ability to make concrete decisions and choices. The rudder allows you to take to the open sea and sail further and further, instead of staying by the shore or bobbing around aimlessly.

Attention and Flexibility

Experienced sailors know their boat. After some time, they know in advance how to react to a given situation. Switching

TRUST YOUR FEELINGS

too quickly to autopilot is not, however, a good idea. The wind can change direction unexpectedly, sometimes gently, sometimes suddenly. Similarly, the desire is not always the same throughout a person's life. It changes. This also applies to the amount of energy available. As with sailing, discerning in everyday life requires constant attention and flexibility to adapt. Otherwise, before you realize it, you risk getting bogged down in *I have always done it this way* or *I have never done it this way*.

3

Practicing Discernment

THE EXAMEN

Discernment is largely dependent on the ability to listen to what is going on inside you. For most people this is not an innate skill. You can, however, learn to connect with your innermost self. Ignatius proposes a simple way of doing this: an Ignatian review of your day, also called an examination of conscience or consciousness. Christians can do this in the presence of and together with God. In this case, the Ignatian review becomes a prayer—the Examen.

Looking Back and Taking Stock

You can look back at the day or the week that has just passed. You can also focus on a particular experience or project, a relationship, or another aspect of your life. Five minutes may be enough. But you can also take a quarter of an hour, half an hour, or more. The individual elements of the Ignatian review were not conceived by Ignatius. But the sequence of the different stages comes from him. It can be summed up in three words: *thanks, sorry,* and *please.*

Listening to your interior world is not easy, especially when it is about becoming aware of your feelings. So, as you begin to look back, take some time to stop and be quiet and, in this way, try to descend to the level of your deepest feelings. Christians can ask God to help them with the review. More specifically, they can ask God to show them when their heart was especially touched.

GIVING THANKS—THANK YOU

The first part of the Examen is the most important: it is about identifying what has brought joy, peace, faith, or other positive feelings. It does not have to be about big highs. Gentle caresses of the heart are also important. It is better to focus on the feeling itself, rather than on the things that caused it. In this way, new, previously unknown experiences can also be brought to the fore, as well as events that you would not automatically expect to leave a good aftertaste.

Positive feelings can be linked to a wide variety of experiences: a particular event at work, what a person said, a song you heard, a religious experience, a work of art you admired, a moment of intimacy between two people on the bus that you witnessed, the peace you felt when distracting music stopped unexpectedly, a friendly salesman in a shop or a waiter in a restaurant, the joy in the eyes of your mother when you paid her an unexpected visit, the pleasant scent of a flower.

You may feel gratitude welling up inside you. For the Christian, this can have a special meaning. After all, you don't thank yourself but rather the one who is the source of the

Practicing Discernment

good that you have received. For the Christian, in the end, it is always God.

Most people have the impulse to start with the negative when they review their experiences. But Ignatius explicitly asks us to start with the positive. In this way, you can gradually become more aware of the presence of life and light in your life. You grow in faith and gratitude. As this awareness develops, it becomes easier and more meaningful to examine the negative feelings.[1]

ASKING FOR FORGIVENESS—SORRY

Saying thank you comes first and is the most important part of the Examen. If there is time left, you can move on to the second stage. The growing feelings of gratitude make it easier (because it is less threatening) to explore places of shadow in your current life. Where or when did you feel sad, angry, bitter, suspicious, apathetic, etcetera?

Here, too, it is advisable to try to become aware first of the inner feelings and only then to see which actions or events led to them. Often, what is going on, insofar as it is down to you, has to do with a refusal, in one way or another, to say yes to life and love in the broadest sense. You may feel sorry for some things and feel the urge to ask for forgiveness.

Negative feelings can be linked to very different experiences: constantly looking at your smartphone during a conversation, your sometimes excessive alcohol consumption, the impatient way you put the children to bed one night, your annoyance in the car in morning traffic, the tone of your response to your son asking for more pocket money, the

---

1. See section, "More light leads to less shadow," page 13.

atmosphere at work lately, your vehemence when discussing politics with friends, your concerns about the division of your parents' inheritance, and so on.

LOOKING TO TOMORROW—PLEASE

If there is still time, in closing you can look to the future. By giving thanks and asking for forgiveness, there is a growing understanding of what is happening in the depths of your being: life and death, light and darkness, presence and absence. What do you do with this information? You could draw from it some resolutions or small changes that you want to work on in the days and weeks ahead. The more concrete these action points, the better. The insights that emerged from the first two stages of the review can serve as a starting point.

You could resolve to say hello to colleagues even if you are generally in a bad mood in the morning; leave the car radio off for fifteen minutes as you drive home in order to review your day; get into the habit of reading a story when it is your turn to put your child to bed; look for another job; apologize to your neighbor for your rude behavior; remove the Facebook app from your smartphone; visit your elderly mother more often.

It can be tempting to want to change many things at the same time. In general, this is not the best approach. It's best to commit yourself to just one or two changes. People take only one step at a time. At the end of the review, you can offer your new resolution to God. You can also ask him for the strength you need to turn your words into action.

Practicing Discernment
THE INNER ANTENNAE

An Ignatian review is most effective if it is done regularly. Practice makes perfect. And this applies also to our inner life. By regularly reviewing your experience, you will fine-tune your inner antennae. The more they are trained, the better equipped you will be to discern inner movements, even those that are hardly perceptible. The small course adjustments they suggest in your daily life make it possible to keep taking steps forward.

4
Discernment and Making Choices

Making the right choice presupposes that you are trying to discover the best way forward in your life. Choice and discernment often go hand in hand. It is not surprising that Ignatius of Loyola gives precise instructions on how to make a good choice. He describes three ways of making a choice.

THE CHOICE THAT FALLS FROM HEAVEN

This first way is not a method. You cannot decide yourself whether to use it or not. It is the choice that, with absolute certainty, falls straight from heaven. It just happens to you, and totally unexpectedly. In a moment, you know what you

Discernment and Making Choices

must do. In fact, you may always have known. It's like an intuition so strong that it's impossible to doubt it, either when it happens or afterward. It's a feeling so strong that it seems that you don't choose but are chosen.

This type of choice is exceptional. Yet it does exist. The sign of it is usually great joy and an absolute certainty about the path to follow. Even afterward, the joyful aftertaste and great certainty remain. Christians see this as a calling, or vocation, and recognize in it the work of God.

> *A well-known and spectacular example is the conversion of the apostle Paul shortly after Jesus's death and resurrection. On the road to Damascus, something inexplicable happened to him. He literally fell to the ground and heard the voice of Jesus. Up to that time, Paul had persecuted the Christians, and yet, in the blink of an eye, he became a fervent Christian. He dedicated the rest of his life to the proclamation of the gospel with incredible energy. He encountered all sorts of resistance and paid for it with his life. And yet, he never questioned his choice.*

CHOOSING ON THE BALANCE OF YOUR FEELINGS

Just as the first way of making a choice is rare, so the second—weighing up your feelings as though on a set of scales—has wide application. It is a method that you can consciously choose and follow. Ignatius of Loyola considers it to be the normal and most reliable method for discerning the right choice. It is a direct application of the basic principles of Ignatian discernment and presupposes, in being relatively elaborate, that the object of the choice has a certain significance.

Weighing up emotions can be used when deciding what to study or whether to have another child, to look for a new job, to move, and to get married or enter religious life. It is used for big choices where there is something real at stake.

Prerequisites

In utilizing this method, it is important, from beginning to end, to ensure your own internal openness and availability.[1] Both are necessary to be able to see what is happening in your heart. If this inner freedom is lacking or insufficient, and you have, in fact, already decided how you want the scales to fall, then it is better not to start. In this case, there can be no real discernment. In other words, don't fix the outcome of the process; leave the choice open. Don't rush things. Give the process time and dare not to know the outcome in advance.

As with any discernment, it is also important in the preparatory phase to gather enough information about the subject in question.[2]

The Importance of an Alternative

Weighing up your feelings requires that you have two equal alternatives between which to choose. You do not choose between something and nothing. You may find that your preference is already moving strongly in a certain direction. Nevertheless, it is still desirable to have a credible second possibility or, if necessary, to create one. Comparison and evaluation become possible because there is an alternative that allows the choice to be approached from a broader perspective. The

---
1. See section, "The Challenge of Inner Availability," page 8.
2. See section, "Using Your Intellect to Prepare the Ground," page 4.

weighing up can then confirm or challenge your more spontaneous feelings. If there is already a strong preference for one option, sincere consideration of another option may help to deepen the choice.

> Anna has had a stable relationship with Pedro for many years. Isn't it time to get married? Anna believes that marriage should be a choice, not something automatic. She wants to make a discernment. Although it is a little artificial, she chooses as an alternative to continue her life without Pedro, with another potential companion.

Two Weeks

We are now ready to begin the process of choosing. It involves two distinct weeks. During the first week, the first option is considered. In the second week, it will be the turn of the alternative. During each of the two weeks, you will lead your normal life, but on the basis that you have chosen that week's option. From time to time, you consciously ask yourself what this means, what your life would look like from now on, what you would and would not do, and so on. You absorb the choice, from morning to night. Regularly, during the day, reflect on what you have been feeling. Have you been calm, confident, joyful, energetic, or, on the contrary, rather anxious, hesitant, empty, irritated, or sad during these hours or the past day? Each time, try to write down what you have noticed in the review.

Result

At the end of each week, take stock. This allows you to see, after two weeks, in which direction the balance of feelings is tilting. Experience shows that this weighing up can bring

TRUST YOUR FEELINGS

more clarity because there is often a noticeable difference between the two weeks. It is often the case that one option is accompanied by more peace, faith, and joy than the other, where more negative feelings may have surfaced.

> *In recent weeks, Anna has been making a discernment about whether to marry Pedro. The result is in line with expectations. At the same time, it surprised her. The comparison lets her see that the prospect of sharing her life with Pedro forever fills her with much more joy than she thought. Conversely, Anna did not realize that a life without Pedro would seem so empty and meaningless to her. Anna feels even more confident about marrying Pedro.*

> *The result may also be different. To her astonishment, Anna might have found that the prospect of a life without Pedro gave her a sense of liberation and a new perspective. This option made her more cheerful and energized than before. Life was beautiful, more beautiful than usual. A whole week with the idea of a life without Pedro made Anna realize that she was suffocating in this relationship and that she hadn't realized it.*

This second method can be used by most people, but not by everyone. Some people have a finely balanced emotional and affective life. Even if there seems to be a reason for emotional fluctuations, they notice few changes in their eversteady heart. It is also possible that for some people, even though weighing up their emotional responses is the right approach, the result itself is not very clear. In these cases, a third method remains, which can also be used to confirm the second method.

Discernment and Making Choices

CHOOSING ON THE BALANCE OF YOUR REASONING

Weighing up what we feel starts with what happens in the heart. Weighing up the facts is rooted in the intellect and reason. It is simply a matter of considering the choice and the alternative very carefully. This explains why the third method for making a choice can be used by everyone. This is especially the case for people who are very calm and have few emotional ups and downs. This method is not, however, entirely objective. Indeed, not everyone will reach the same conclusion by dealing with these issues in a rational way.

Prerequisites

To be able to weigh up the facts, the same prerequisite applies as for weighing up feelings. Indeed, this method makes sense only if you have sufficient inner freedom and openness to consider and analyze the issue rationally and calmly.[3] This is something to pay particular attention to from the beginning to the end of the process.

Here again, you cannot make a blind discernment. In other words, you must have enough information—who, what, where, how, how much, etcetera?—before the weighing up begins.[4]

What Questions?

In these cases, a broad range of questions can be addressed: from fundamental life choices to purely practical and material issues of ordinary life and everything in between.

---
3. See section, "The Challenge of Inner Availability," page 8.
4. See section, "Using Your Intellect to Prepare the Ground," page 4.

TRUST YOUR FEELINGS

It is important that the question is formulated precisely and that it is possible to answer it with a yes or no answer.

This third method can be used for questions such as the choice of life partner, studies, career, moving to a different city, holiday destination, buying a new car, or joining a sports club.

In contrast to weighing up feelings, weighing up facts does not really need an alternative. If you do have one or more alternatives, however, you can still use this method.

Arguments For and Against

In weighing up facts, you take the proposal: I'm going to join this sports club. You write down all the arguments you can think of, for and against, each in its own column. These arguments can be objective, material, or more subjective and emotional. You should not limit yourself to high-minded or politically correct arguments. Very practical and down-to-earth considerations are also welcome. It is meant to be done rather quickly. You can also choose, if you wish, to do the same thing with the opposite position: I'm not going to join this sports club. So, you get two or four columns with lists of arguments for and arguments against.

Arguments for	Arguments against
My doctor strongly advises me to do so	Membership is expensive
It is near my home	I won't go very often
Some of my friends also work out there	I don't have enough time
I like the decor and the light	I don't like sport

Discernment and Making Choices

Evaluate

After making an inventory, you will weigh up the various arguments for and against. The idea is to consider each of the arguments and to assess the relative importance you give to each of them. The aim is to use your intelligence primarily but also your heart. What do the purely rational arguments provoke in terms of an emotional response? If it helps, you can give a number to each argument, for example, from 1 (not important) to 10 (very important). Finally, you can work out, by weighing up or calculating the direction in which the scale is tilting.

This third method can also be used to deepen or confirm a choice made according to the second method. It can happen that the results of these two methods are opposite. The heart and the mind do not always point in the same direction. In this case, it is important to realize that the heart is more attuned to what is personal and intimate than reason, which by definition is impersonal and therefore more neutral. The weight of the heart can therefore be greater than that of more abstract reasoning. In short, the power and reliability of an emotional weighing up is greater than that of pure reasoning.

> *William is a research scientist. He is being offered tenure and a significant promotion. If he accepts, he knows that his future within the research center is guaranteed. He will also earn a lot more money. His current position is uncertain. Because of his high degree of specialization, William sees few other job opportunities for himself. Accepting this promotion means, however, that he will be given more management responsibilities and that he will have to say*

goodbye to the laboratory for good. For William's colleagues it seems obvious that he should choose promotion. Weighing up the facts tips the balance in that direction. But the balance of his emotions is the other way around. William is passionate about research. It is his life. If he gives it up, too much of who he is will die.

TWO MORE TIPS

It may be that, when weighing up the facts, you find it difficult because of some bias not to give an answer too quickly. To remedy this and to sharpen your inner availability, Ignatius proposes two additional exercises.

You can also imagine that you have to give advice to a complete stranger on the very same subject about which you are making a choice. What would you recommend to this person?

You can imagine lying on your deathbed. What choice would you hope to have made, from this specific perspective, in relation to the question at hand?

In both cases, the idea is to take a little more distance when considering your situation. Then, hopefully with more objectivity and inner freedom, you can turn to the question again using the method of rationally weighing the facts.

5
Discernment and Education

Ignatian discernment can make a valuable contribution to the education of children and young people.

Children and young people want to discover who and what they are. They want to experiment and grow. The unknown attracts them greatly. Pushing boundaries and reaching beyond yourself is a source of pleasure. It can take much effort, but it gives you even more energy. This is how our personalities gradually grow.

For some people, this quest continues throughout life. Others seem to get bogged down quickly in gray mediocrity. The desire for life leads some people to become more human and welcoming. For others, however, this journey seems to degenerate quickly into an insatiable thirst for ever more power, money, and personal glory. Is this simply chance? Or is it instead a way of being in the world and therefore something that can be learned?

Ignatian spirituality and pedagogy go hand in hand. They offer valuable advice to parents and educators to guide children and young people in their quest and growth toward being more fully human. In this search for their vocation, discernment can play an important role. Three central elements are addressed here.

EACH PATH OF GROWTH IS UNIQUE

The path of growth in each human being is unique. Children and young people often tend to compare themselves to each other and want to outdo each other. This is not a problem provided it does not make us forget that each person's path is unique. Every human being is called to shape their own way of being human and, in doing so, to discover their own strengths.

For some, it will be more at the level of relationships; for others, it will be at the artistic, intellectual, religious, or sporting level, or simply at the level of the ordinary things of everyday life.

The invitation to growth is addressed to everyone, whatever the richness or the limits of their capacities. No one is predestined to mediocrity. A good education is one that gives the child or young person the opportunity to experience the joy of growth, however modest it may be.

THE DEEPEST PERSONAL DESIRE TO GROW

The unique path of growth is linked to the deepest personal desire to grow. It is not a question of inventing your own vocation. Nor is it a good idea to choose it in the supermarket of ever-changing fashions. That will not bring any real satisfaction. Your true vocation is received. It has everything to do with your deepest personal desire. A true vocation comes from within.

Special Responsibility for Educators

To connect with this deep desire, it is important that children and young people can get in touch with their inner self. In doing so, they can discover that their concrete experiences also leave a mark at the level of their deepest feelings. These are important because they can point the way to those things that make us truly happy or, conversely, that prevent us from living life to the fullest.

The key tool here is the review. Therefore, it is important to invite the child or young person to reflect regularly on their experiences in a way that is adapted to their age. By articulating their inner feelings, they also become more aware of them. Consequently, they learn to appreciate more fully the importance and significance of their lived experience.

For example, what has this activity, this meeting, this book, this subject at school, this trip, this recent holiday provoked in you, in the moment and afterward? What makes you happy at this point in your life? Where do you feel strength, energy, and passion? What gives you peace and confidence? The more difficult or problematic side of life can be highlighted by questions such as: What made you uncomfortable, anxious, or sad? What seemed attractive at first but eventually left you feeling empty and dissatisfied?

Educators have a particular responsibility in this regard. The sooner and more often the child is given the opportunity to (learn to) discern, the better. For a five-year-old child, the approach will be different from that for a fifteen-year-old teenager, but it is equally important for both.

In this way, a child or young person can gradually become aware of what really warms their heart or makes it beat. Conversely, they may also become more aware of what makes them frustrated and unsettled. The wider the range of experiences that can be reflected on, the more informative and relevant will the review be.

> *One Sunday morning I was at the train station to catch a train. The train had just arrived. Right in front of me, a young father wanted to get on the train with his six- or seven-year-old son. The step to get into the carriage was too high and too far from the platform for the child. The father stretched out his arm and the boy held on to it. In this way, the father was able to pull his child into the carriage. Once in the train, the boy turned around to look at his father with a radiant smile: "Thank you, Daddy, for helping me get on the train." Obviously, this child had already learned at a very early age to pay attention to what was going on in his heart and to express it.*

Finally, it is a good thing to let the child or young person experience, in an age-appropriate way, that they can truly let their choices, big and small, be inspired by deep personal desires. To the extent that their choices are inspired by their deepest desires, a great source of energy is released. If you are on the right path, you will find, or be given, the strength to walk it. In this way, the child or young person can grow step by step to become the beautiful person he or she is called to be.

Discernment and Education

AN AUTHENTIC PATH OF GROWTH LEADS TO OTHERS

The first two points are very much "I" focused. They might give the impression that an Ignatian-inspired education is a license to spend a lifetime polishing the work of art that is the self. This may seem satisfying at times. But in the end, such an attitude leads only to a dead end. Human experience, in general, and the gospel, in particular, point in a different direction. Human beings can become truly happy only to the extent that they are gradually freed from the need always to put themselves at the center.

To become fully human, a person must learn to look beyond their own interests and make room for the other. The joy they can then experience is the deepest joy there is. People become fully human only when they can give themselves to others. Children and young people have a right to be able to discover this. It is therefore the duty of parents and educators to make it possible.

In Ignatian-inspired schools, it has been common practice for several decades to ask young people to volunteer for and with those who live on the margins of our society. This regular commitment is accompanied by a process of reviewing. Young people discover, often to their great astonishment, that commitment to others brings them greater joy than anything they have experienced before. Many report that this experience is one of the strongest in their schooling and that it has influenced their choice of studies and career.

6

Discerning between Right and Wrong

Not all pleasant feelings point us in the right direction. Not all unpleasant feelings point us in the wrong direction. Ignatian discernment is much more subtle than this. This is particularly true of Ignatius's analysis of the workings of good and evil. On the one hand, what may be surprising is that the dynamic of evil usually begins with a pleasant feeling and is therefore initially appealing. The dynamic of good, on the other hand, often meets with resistance in the beginning. The result for each, of course, is the opposite.

THE DYNAMIC OF EVIL

Evil, also called the devil, is a mysterious force that wants to destroy humanity. *The enemy of human nature* or *Lucifer*, as Ignatius sometimes calls evil, tries to isolate people from each other, to lock them up within themselves, and thus to keep them away from genuine living. Ignatius teaches that evil sometimes presents itself in a very benign or attractive way. In this mode, it takes the form of the *angel of light*.[1] Starting from something good and pleasant, it uses cunning to try to damage a person's very humanity by disrupting their relationships. This applies to individuals but also to the community. Evil works in two different ways that seem to be opposed but that are nevertheless close to each other. Both are based on an overvaluation of wealth, in the broadest sense of the term.

The Path of Consistently Overestimating Yourself

Ignatius of Loyola sums up this way of doing evil in three words: riches, arrogance, pride.

Riches

The dynamics of evil put wealth first. Anyone who possesses a lot of money, knowledge, wisdom, relationships, influence, power, or prestige can accomplish much. You can do everything on your own because you have the necessary know-how "in house." This makes it possible to avoid being reliant on others. After all, what you do yourself, you do better.

This logic suggests that someone who has, knows, and can do a lot is simply worth more. Instead of being a means, wealth can become an end. It is then obvious that you will strive to obtain more and more wealth. This can easily lead you to start identifying with this success and wealth. It feels good, gives you confidence, and brings satisfaction. You feel completely in control.

---

[1]. See section, "The evil angel who turns into an angel of light," page 38.

TRUST YOUR FEELINGS

From riches to arrogance

If you ask yourself why you are doing so well, the answer seems clear. It's because of you, yourself—your studies, your work, your creativity, and all your other talents. Wealth did not come by itself. It was achieved first and foremost by your own merit. But why is it not the same for others? Among them, there are many who also do their best. A small voice whispers the answer: You are better than the others.

From riches, through arrogance, to pride

Thus, the logic of placing too much emphasis on wealth ultimately leads to pride. You believe that you are better than others. You are simply the best. Of course, you are not going to shout it from the rooftops, but secretly, you don't think it's a crazy idea. You don't really need others. After all, you are more accomplished than them. Gradually, you begin to see yourself as the center of your family, your group of friends, your business, your school, and your community.

Riches have led you to see reality as a pyramid. You are at the top. From these heights, you look down, condescendingly, at all those people who are inferior. Truly collaborating or doing things with others is no longer interesting. They don't offer you anything. After all, you are better than them. What's more, these others have gradually become afraid of the harsh and distant person you've become. You may be at the top. But at the top, there is room for only one. Pride has turned you into someone solitary and unapproachable. You are a prisoner of your wealth. The false logic that has given too much value to wealth has cut you off from your fellow human beings. In the depths of your heart, you are unhappy. You appear successful, but as a human being, and therefore as a relational being, you are somehow dead.

Discerning between Right and Wrong

The Path of Consistently Underestimating Yourself

The overvaluing of riches can also lead to an inverse dynamic, that of consistently underestimating yourself. This seems very different. Nevertheless, it leads to a similar end point as the dynamic of overestimating yourself: breaking off relationships with the people around you.

Denial of self-worth

You realize that there are many qualities you don't have: you're not the brightest or the wisest; you're not as sociable as you would like; and you don't express yourself very fluently. Instead of believing that you are great, you think that you are nothing. The more you think about it, the clearer it becomes that you are worthless. What you can do and what you have, it seems, does not outweigh what you can't do and don't have. These ideas become fixed. If something succeeds or goes well, it's considered a coincidence or a mistake. A word of encouragement from a friend or colleague can be inspired only by pity.

From denial of self-worth to feeling inferior

There's no doubt about it: you are an inferior being. You are locked up in the dungeon of your limits, and you are your own jailer. You are the only one with the key. The last thing you will do, however, is use that key. There is only a small step between *I can do nothing* and *I am nothing*. You consider yourself irrelevant, awkward, as good as dead, isolated from others, and without value or dignity.

TRUST YOUR FEELINGS

This mindset is particularly common among young people. Nevertheless, even adults can find themselves trapped in this logic.

From denial of self-worth, through feeling inferior, to self-destruction

The thought of suicide—or at least separating yourself from the company of others—seems to be a logical conclusion. Other forms of (self-)destructive behavior are also part of this dynamic: eating or drinking too much or too little, behaving violently, or, conversely, being overly passive. Once again, evil hides under the appearance of good. After all, ceasing to exist or withdrawing from social life will bring peace and tranquility to yourself and others.

Here again, the result is that the relationship with neighbor and self is severely disrupted, as is the possibility of relationship with God: *How could I ever face him?* The overvaluing of riches—this time in the form of not having certain things—has completely undermined your humanity.

In contrast to the first variant, here there is a negative feeling from beginning to end. This does not prevent this dynamic from having a powerful attraction.

THE DYNAMIC OF GOOD

The dynamic of evil undermines relationships. The dynamic of good does the opposite. Here too, three stages can be identified. At first glance, they do not seem all that appealing. For many, they provoke resistance. In the end, however, they lead to deep joy. In this dynamic, Christians recognize the essence of the evangelical life of Jesus.

Discerning between Right and Wrong

Limitations

The dynamic of good begins from the experience of human beings as limited and imperfect. If you look honestly at your life, you can see that there are many things that you cannot do or are not proud of. Human beings, no matter how talented, constantly come up against their limits. Time runs out. The unexpected can throw a spanner in the works. There is so much that you would like to do and yet so little that you manage to do. It can hurt and sometimes make you very unhappy.

One of the limitations is that you often find that you can't do something on your own. People need others, even if they would prefer to do it themselves. These other people, in turn, have limits and weaknesses. The same applies to the organizations and structures in which we live and work. It is enough to make you lose courage.

Limitation and confrontation

Most people naturally prefer to avoid facing up to this helplessness and the many limitations of our world. To do the opposite can take much courage. Awareness of what is not or cannot be done is painful. It is challenging. It brings you firmly back down to earth. No sane person likes this sometimes-brutal encounter with harsh reality.

For Ignatius, the willingness and audacity to confront this human smallness and powerlessness is a crucial step in the dynamic of the good. Christians are not always aware of this, but in the life of Jesus, this painful confrontation occupies a central place. It could have been avoided. But Jesus deliberately did not do so. Think, for example, of his experiences of disbelief, injustice, selfishness, stubbornness, rejection, false accusations, cowardice, ignorance, failure, illness, and death. Christians see the culmination of this confrontation, the crucifixion and all that accompanies it, as the core and essence of his message. Through the cross of Jesus, people have gradually come to understand that this abject human poverty can become a gateway to the fullness of life and the love of God.

This means that we, ordinary people, do not have to be afraid of this reality, however painful it may be. This confrontation always comes at the wrong time and often strikes where we don't want it to. The experience of Jesus, however, shows that it is possible to live with this limitation and helplessness in such a way that these, too, can become a gateway to greater joy. The result of such a difficult confrontation with our fundamental poverty can be a growing openness and ability to receive.

From limitation, through confrontation, to receptivity

Being able to receive means accepting that you don't have to have everything or be able to do everything. Being open in this way allows you to be at peace with the fact that you are limited as a person or as a group and that you do not control everything that happens. The receptive person can, and wants to, be open to receive the help of others. Being receptive means that you can and want to receive, not just to give.

Working together, making compromises, and experiencing your own weakness, limitation, and dependency will no longer be a failure. The other is no longer a rival to whom you must prove yourself, but rather someone you can trust, someone with whom you can experience life and its beauty. Receptivity leads to the discovery that everything of value in life is ultimately a gift. You cannot really give until you have first learned to receive.

Being able to receive makes gratitude and wonder possible. Receptivity is the experience that it is the other who makes you grow. For Christians, the other, in the end, is God. Receptivity is the source and condition of joy par excellence. It takes away your hard edges and opens the way to humor and healthy self-mockery. Receptivity means that imperfection is no longer seen as an obstacle. Rather, it is an invitation to enter into relationship with each other and to receive and learn from each other.

Spiritual Pedagogy

The dynamic of the good that Ignatius distills from the example of Jesus is a particular spiritual pedagogy that allows us to confront the dark side of human life. It makes it possible not to passively endure human limitation as a tragic fate. It teaches that we should not be afraid or ashamed of being confronted with our own poverty or that of others through the destabilizing experience of incapacity, failure, or injustice. There is no need to repress or rationalize these experiences. They can be acknowledged and seen as a possible path to more authentic humanity. Thus, the experience of our limits can ultimately lead to deep joy and become a path to greater happiness.

The dynamics of good and evil remain present in us throughout our lives. The dynamic of evil is sometimes very subtle. It can be disconcerting to discover the extent to which evil can manipulate us. Behind seemingly noble motives, there can indeed be something devious at work. With these two dynamics, Ignatius offers an interpretive framework that can help us to discern what is ultimately good and bad. They are precious tools for growing in authenticity in our lives.

7
Discerning in Particular Situations

Life can confront us with a wide variety of experiences and situations. Ignatius's expertise can help us discern what is good and useful in diverse circumstances. Ten specific situations are presented below, along with advice on how best to discern. What is noteworthy with this advice is that it often recommends doing the opposite of what we would normally want to do.

WHEN YOU ARE IN SEVENTH HEAVEN

With joyful experiences, Ignatius recommends treating differently the experience itself and the inner feelings that

Discerning in Particular Situations

accompany it, on the one hand, and the thoughts that may arise from the experience, on the other. An experience that brings you happiness and peace, not only in the moment but also over time, is reliable. We have already seen that being left with a good aftertaste is usually a sign that this is something that will lead to more rather than less life.[1] You can be confident from this that what has happened on this occasion is real and significant for you. It may be a good idea, afterward, to chew over the experience again to draw more joy and strength from it.

Ignatius, however, warns against thoughts and plans that may emerge after such a strong experience. They do not always have the same degree of trustworthiness as the experience itself and the positive feelings that accompany it. They can be reliable, but sometimes they are not. They need to be examined in more detail before they are acted on.

> *Susan's relationship with her adult son, Victor, has been seriously damaged. A calm conversation has not been possible for a long time. Mother and son rarely see each other. There is a lot of anger and mutual pain. On her birthday, Susan made another attempt. She invited Victor to a nice restaurant. For the first time in years, they were able to talk to each other without arguing. At first, both were suspicious, but the ice melted quickly. It was hesitant and fragile. Yet Susan felt a new openness and good will. They left each other relieved and happy. In the days that followed, Susan continued to feel grateful and hopeful. She finds it hard to believe. Yet she considers that what happened at that dinner was true.*

---

[1]. See section, "Aftertaste," page 34.

TRUST YOUR FEELINGS

Susan has a strong desire to normalize the relationship with her son quickly. Enough time has already been wasted and she has so much to tell Victor. Wouldn't it be a good idea to suggest that they have lunch together every week from now on?

Susan can rely on the good aftertaste that the dinner and conversation with Victor have left. Hope is justified. Nevertheless, she should carefully consider the plan that emerged so spontaneously in the days that followed. It may well be the case that, even though it is well intentioned, her idea will have the opposite effect from the one she hopes.

WHEN YOU ARE ANGRY

In the case of anger, too, Ignatius distinguishes between the feelings associated with an experience and the thoughts that accompany them. The advice he gives in this case is the exact opposite of the previous situation.

Experiences that make you angry, annoyed, hard, and bitter at the time, and afterward, do not usually point in a direction that leads to more life. It is better not to keep going back to them in your memory or to allow the negativity to reinvade your heart later. There is nothing good there. Righteous anger exists,[2] but it is rare. It is better to try to let go of anger and bitterness. The risk of getting stuck and drowning in it is too high.

Lucifer's Thoughts

Ignatius, however, points out that thoughts and plans that arise mainly out of anger must be treated differently

---

2. See section, "Righteous anger," page 39.

Discerning in Particular Situations

from anger itself. Experience shows that these thoughts are often relevant. In the Bible, the devil is sometimes called the accuser. The accuser sees people's mistakes and rightly denounces them. The devil is also called Lucifer. Lucifer literally means light-bearer. Lucifer brings the light of truth. He tells the truth about the people he meets. Specifically, he mentions their faults. Jesus does this too, but it is so that people can learn and become better people. The devil does it out of wickedness and to cause damage.

> *George discovers that his daughter, Effy, has lied again. This time it was a big one. She has completely betrayed his trust. George is furious. He sees very clearly how this tendency to lie has become a habit for Effy. Her lack of self-confidence means that when things get harder, she prefers to run away from the truth rather than face it. Things cannot go on like this.*

Double Victory

The automatic response may be to confront the person concerned with this truth. George could angrily accuse Effy of lying. But the effect is then likely to be the opposite of what he wants. The girl will simply experience his anger and, naturally enough, will seek to protect herself from it. The result will be that the *truth*, which Effy needs to hear, will not come out. But the rage might hit home. Such an angry reprimand risks locking the girl in her problem or mistake rather than freeing her.

> *Effy might say to herself after her father's anger: "I am a cowardly liar, but I'm going to continue lying*

TRUST YOUR FEELINGS

because I'm not brave enough to take responsibility. Dad knows me perfectly well. He is right."

The victory of evil is twofold. The constructive and corrective potential of the truth is lost. What's more, Effy is not delivered from but confirmed in her error. George has been able to discharge his anger, but it is his daughter who pays the price.

Choosing to Postpone

How do you deal constructively with this *truth* revealed by anger? Ignatius recommends using the insights and thoughts, but not right away. He suggests waiting until the anger has subsided, and you have calmed down. Then you can consider the insights again, now, no longer out of anger, but rather out of love and concern for the other person. In this way, they will no longer be destructive accusations but rather an invitation to move forward.

A few days after Effy's lie, George has calmed down. Instead of anger, he now feels love again for his little girl, who does not always have an easy life. He invites her to join him for an ice cream. She loves it. Then they go for a walk, and he talks quietly about the incident. He doesn't hesitate to tell Effy how his father helped him to stop lying when he was small. At the end of the walk, they give each other a big hug. George is happy that he bit his tongue a few days earlier.

When you can look at the person in question again in a positive light, it's time to start the conversation. There is now a real chance that even a difficult message will be received. After all,

Discerning in Particular Situations

when you feel loved, trust increases, together with the ability to let yourself be challenged even in your places of vulnerability. You know then with your heart that the person is not against you but for you. By engaging in such conversation, you are doing the person concerned a valuable service. Provided you are patient, you allow them to grow as a human being.

WHEN YOU ARE UNHAPPY

Ignatius of Loyola assumes that feelings such as joy, peace, and trust are normal. At the same time, experience teaches us that feelings such as sadness, disillusionment, emptiness, and apathy occur more often than we would like. Therefore, Ignatius makes suggestions for dealing with them in a way that promotes rather than hinders the return of positive feelings.

An Invitation to Deepen and Purify

It's good to feel peace, trust, and tenderness. But a person can also be without these positive feelings. Furthermore, something good can come from sadness or dismay. You can see them as an invitation to distinguish what is essential from what is incidental and thus get closer to what is fundamental in your life.

> *Olivia goes to see her mother twice a day. She does everything she can for her mother who can no longer live independently. The old lady cannot accept this yet. Her helplessness often makes her aggressive toward Olivia. Hugh, her favorite son, comes to visit every fortnight. In the days that follow, Olivia hears time and again how sweet and attentive Hugh is. A*

word of thanks for Olivia rarely comes to her mother's lips. This is very painful for Olivia. In the beginning, she often reacted with harsh words. Lately, she has noticed that she is becoming more patient with her mother. She feels that her love for her mother is getting stronger again, even if it doesn't seem to be reciprocated. Olivia is grateful for this. She feels that the experience with her mother, as painful as it is, is moving her forward.

It is good to realize that it is not inevitable that you will get swept away by these negative feelings. Sadness and disillusionment do not necessarily have to lead you into a negative spiral. Reflecting on what exactly is going on in the heart can help you to detect traces of new confidence and hope as quickly as possible.

Taking the Initiative to Turn the Tide

It is characteristic of negative feelings that they can cause you to slip back into superficiality and laziness. Ignatius advises, in these moments of sadness, to do more, even though our natural inclination is to do less.

You then consciously choose to go against your gut reaction, because you know, on a deeper level, that this can open the way to the return of your zest for life. This can start with practical and simple things.

Francine got of the bed out on the wrong side today and has little motivation. She knows that, for her, things can easily go from bad to worse. Experience has taught her that in such a situation it helps her to clean her office, do some ironing, or deadhead the

Discerning in Particular Situations

roses in the garden. These are small, meaningful jobs that require little effort or concentration and are "safe" because they can't really fail. When Francine has done this, even if she is in a bad mood, it always gives her satisfaction and can be a springboard to more.

By working consciously on yourself in this way, you can be better equipped to deal with negativity. Ignatius gives four concrete tips on how to take the initiative yourself to turn the tide on negative feelings.

Silence and Prayer

When things don't go well, he begins, we often tend to take less time for silence, prayer, and meditation. Ignatius recommends the opposite. If things are difficult, you should drink more at the source, not less. Perhaps you need to opt for a different and more suitable form of spiritual food than you are used to. Cutting yourself off from your roots leads nowhere.

For some time now, Martin has been feeling bad about himself. He is not very happy at work. Over the last few months, his relationship with his girlfriend has deteriorated. Martin has no idea where this unhappiness is coming from. He used to read the Bible regularly and go to church from time to time, but he has stopped doing this. In any case, the silence only made him more confused. As soon as he gets home, he puts his music on loud. One day, he opens up to Jennifer, a colleague. Martin knows that she is a good listener. During the conversation, he realizes how important contact with nature has

> *always been to him. Curiously, he has completely stopped walking in the forest. From then on, he decides to resume his weekly forest walks. He also downloads a meditation app to allow himself to experience silence and prayer from time to time.*

This also applies to other important sources of nourishment and relationships that can bring you closer to the essentials of life. When things get complicated with your partner or with your wider family or closest friends, it may well be a sign that you simply need to invest more in these relationships. Sitting back and waiting for the problem to pass, or seeking happiness elsewhere, will not help.

Reflecting on Your Day

The natural reaction could also be *I'm not going to worry too much or ask myself difficult questions*. Ignatius's second piece of advice again goes in the opposite direction. He encourages you to take more time to look back and reflect on what is going on. This will help you to understand better what is really happening and what, in your lifestyle or environment, may be contributing to the negative feelings. In this review, you can also look for what is still giving you, despite everything, some peace and feelings of trust or openness. You may then discover that these are occurring in ways that you are not used to or in places you would not have expected.

> *Catherine retired recently. It's a tough transition. She now volunteers a lot and spends more time with her grandchildren. Nevertheless, she still misses contact with her patients. She feels that what she does now is just a nice way to keep busy. On the*

Discerning in Particular Situations

internet, she reads an article on the Examen prayer.[3] *After some hesitation, Catherine decides to take ten minutes each evening to review her day. She looks for everything that has given her joy and is astonished. She soon discovers that her volunteer work with the refugees and the time given to her grandchildren are giving her much more satisfaction than she thought. She also notices that the calmer pace of her new life suits her very well. Could it be that her retirement is not such a bad thing?*

Reducing Excesses

Ignatius's third tip is also contrary to what you would most naturally do. Material prosperity, a good network of friends, interesting hobbies, good food and drink, a varied and relaxing life are all good things, but you can get lost in them. All the great spiritual traditions refer to abstinence and simplicity as tools to get closer to the essentials of life.

Thomas and Annette feel that they have found the right rhythm. They both have a full professional life. On weekends, they regularly go to the cinema or theatre. They also like to go to dinner with friends. They are also both very sporty. In the summer, they enjoy a well-deserved exotic holiday. Annette and Thomas would like to have children, but they have not yet found the time. Annette is increasingly busy. For some time, she feels that there has been a certain heaviness in her relationship with Thomas. It's starting to worry her. The first idea that comes to her is that she just needs to organize more creative activities with interesting people. Annette asks her

---

3. See chapter 3, "Practicing Discernment."

> *mother for advice. To her great surprise, she recommends that they go out not more but less. She and Thomas could simply do nothing from time to time, be together, and learn to talk again about what touches their hearts.*

It could well be that feelings of discomfort or dismay are a signal that you are losing yourself in the abundance of your rich and busy life. It might be a good idea to create more space or emptiness again to make more room for what really matters.

Patience

Finally, Ignatius's fourth tip is that feelings of sadness will always want you to believe that they are never going to go away—it's part of what they are. The whole future becomes bleak. It can seem that things will never get better.

The popular saying that there is sunshine after the rain contains a deep wisdom. In other words, it is important to be patient. If you have already begun to put the first three pieces of advice into practice, then you can have even greater confidence that the sadness will not last.

These four concrete tips show how it is possible to turn the corner on negative feelings. For the Christian, this goes straight to the heart of Christian hope and faith. God never abandons us. He writes straight with our curved lines. Experience shows, however, that in some circumstances, the call to be patient and to trust is often not enough because the attraction of negative feelings can be great.

Discerning in Particular Situations

WHEN YOU ARE AFRAID

A particular variant of sadness is fear. Fear can literally freeze a person and cut them off from life. There is something compelling about fear. It has a natural tendency to grow and take up all the space. The reason is simple. It is part of fear to put forward all sorts of relevant arguments, often difficult to refute, to explain why apocalyptic scenarios will necessarily become reality. It therefore seems normal and inevitable that you feel fear. Thus, fear feeds and reinforces itself and can become obsessive.

> *Leo, a final-year nursing student, has chosen to specialize in cardiology. He is starting his first internship. From the very first day, he must perform many difficult tasks. But things aren't going well. The work in cardiology must be done quickly and with great precision because it is very technical. His supervisor makes several negative comments. Leo feels increasingly anxious and insecure. "This internship is not going well. I'm not up to it. I'm sure I'll get a very bad evaluation." At the end of the day, the young man is exhausted and completely panicked. It is obvious to him that he has made the wrong choice with his specialization.*

Of all the negative emotional movements, fear is perhaps the most destructive. Yet it is not very difficult to stop it in its tracks. Four key tools may be helpful in this regard.

TRUST YOUR FEELINGS

Express Yourself

It is important not to keep fear to yourself but to talk about it. Fear grows best in secrecy. Talking about fear with someone you trust can be an important first step. It can help to break the self-perpetuating logic of fear. It is, however, essential that the person you are speaking to neither confirms nor reinforces the fear.

Examine the Facts

A second tool can be to critically examine the facts behind the fear. Often the perception of these facts is confused, incorrect, or incomplete; wrong connections are made and wrong conclusions are drawn, hence their anxiety-provoking effect. The experience just described is perhaps the ideal opportunity to bring more objectivity and calm.

> *In the evening, Leo calls a nurse friend who also works in cardiology. From the conversation, it appears that Leo has indeed made several mistakes, even if they don't seem that serious. The discussion also makes Leo realize, to his surprise, that he has done a lot of things right. Maybe cardiology is not such a bad choice after all.*

Fear Deceives

The third piece of advice is the most important and fundamental. The strength of fear lies above all in the conviction that it is justified. Fear can present subtle and relevant arguments like no other. They aim to strengthen the credibility of fear. You honestly believe that you are right to feel anxious. The arguments put forward prove that you have no choice but to be afraid.

Discerning in Particular Situations

This is exactly where fear's deception lies. It is true that, from time to time, what we are afraid of does in fact happen. You should not, however, be frightened of this. You can deal with problems. That's what you do from morning to night.

> *It's true that Leo's course didn't start very well. It could hardly be otherwise. Cardiology is a difficult specialization. It is normal for someone new not to be very effective at the beginning, even if they are doing their best. This applies to Leo as well as to the other students. The learning curve for an internship like this is usually very steep. Leo can be assured that this will still be the case for him in a few weeks' time.*

Fear Is an Obstacle to Living in the Present

A fourth point concerns the fact that fear is often linked to problems, whether imagined or not, that take place in some vague future. One insidious consequence of anxiety about a future that does not yet exist is that it prevents people from living to the max in a present that does exist. Here, too, speaking to someone can offer release.

> *Jade, a young teenage girl, is crying in bed. When her mother comes to say goodnight, she tells her what is happening. Jade is afraid her friends will turn their backs on her one day. There is no evidence for such a thing, yet the girl is in the grip of fear. The short conversation with her mother quickly brings Jade back to peace.*

Fear is a bad counsellor. It is not good to follow fear's false logic. It is wise not to dialogue with fear and wise also to choose consciously to have faith in the future. The path to a richer and more abundant life is indicated by faith and hope, not by fear. It is not for nothing that Jesus keeps on saying: *Do not be afraid.*

WHEN YOU ARE IN CRISIS

In this context, crisis is an experience of impasse that is perceived as problematic. The crisis is often accompanied by a chaotic succession of contradictory feelings. As with sadness, Ignatius suggests here that you should not do what might seem most natural.

Standing Firm

When you are in crisis, you generally want to get out of it as quickly as possible. Ignatius's advice on this subject is the exact opposite. In times of crisis, it is better to hold back from making choices. He advises, as far as possible, not to change anything. It is better to stick to the decisions you made before—when you were calm and you had your bearings. Choices made in those circumstances are more reliable than any hasty changes you might make now. Do not question, therefore, the decisions you made before. Wait until you are back in calmer waters. At that point, you will be able to discern what to do.

> *Jules is facing a serious conflict in the office. He is turned inside out by it. He would like to take drastic decisions right away to change things. He realizes, however, that his current emotions are like a yo-yo. In the morning, he feels apathetic; at noon, he's scared; and in the evening, he's furious. The nightmares he's*

having at night don't help him either. To tell the truth, Jules doesn't really know where he stands any more, let alone what the best thing for him to do would be.

WHEN YOU DON'T FEEL ANYTHING

Sometimes, you don't feel anything, not even in important relationships or commitments about which you usually have strong feelings.

Charlotte and David are married. They love each other very much and have for many years. Sometimes, Charlotte doesn't feel anything for David. The first few times, she found it strange. Now she doesn't worry about it anymore. It's just what happens.

A priest, a pastor, or a nun may realize that from time to time, everything to do with faith and God leaves them cold and doesn't have any meaning for them, at least at that moment. When this happens to them, they have learned to go on with their lives and their commitments, as if nothing is wrong.

Because deep feelings are very reliable, you don't always need them, and you can do without them for a while. How can that be so?

Building on Previous Feelings

Experience tells us that some feelings can be very strong; at other times, they can be much weaker or even completely absent. This is not necessarily a problem. You can go on quietly living your life; there is no reason to panic. You have the right not to feel anything. That is part of life. It does not mean that you immediately need to question your marriage or other commitments. After all, you have had the experience before, deep in your soul, that tells you it was, and is, good. And this you can continue to trust. The present period of silence does not invalidate the previous experience.

In a broader sense, a person has the right to feel down sometimes. Joy is desirable. But this does not mean that you should give in to the dictatorship of feeling good. Feeling good all the time, however pleasant it may be, is not essential.

WHEN YOU HAVE A PROBLEM

You are experiencing a serious problem at work, an impossible conflict, a traumatic experience, a hopeless relationship, or something similar. This situation demands a great investment of time, energy, and attention, especially because it makes you very agitated, angry, or anxious. It has taken hold of your life in such a way that, as soon as you stop, it draws all your attention, so that it becomes hard to listen to what your heart is saying about other important issues in your life.

The Principle of the Refrigerator

The refrigerator principle can bring relief here. It means that you consciously choose to put the problem in the fridge for a period so that it can cool down. You let yourself forget about it for a while. The refrigerator principle can be beneficial and liberating for several reasons.

Discerning in Particular Situations

> *Lauren, along with other members of her family, has received an inheritance from a rich uncle. The joy doesn't last long. Sharing leads to fierce quarrels. Lawyers are involved, the dispute goes to court. Lauren no longer sleeps. Day and night, she is haunted by this cursed inheritance. What's more, the case is hopelessly deadlocked. Lauren decides to forget the case for the next six months. Within a few days, she is back on her feet and is enjoying the little things again. After six months, Lauren notices that she has adopted a much calmer attitude toward the dispute. For the first time, the idea comes to her that she could propose a compromise to the other heirs. Lauren is now ready to find common ground.*

Consciously letting go for a period can make you realize that you are not obliged to devote all your time and attention to one problem, even if this had been the situation in the past. You rediscover other important things in your life. You realize again that there are also good things and wonderful people around you that you had almost forgotten existed. You can once again offer them time and attention, without feeling guilty for not devoting yourself full-time to this unfortunate issue. Strength and joy return, and there is space in your life for creativity and new initiatives.

Relief

You may also have noticed that lately you have not really been able to pray. Everything was focused on this one concern. By sticking the concern in the fridge, as it were, you are giving yourself permission to open your antenna more widely again in prayer. What a relief!

TRUST YOUR FEELINGS

Experience shows that, after a while, when you take the problem out of the fridge, things really can have changed. Sometimes the problem seems to have evaporated. Obsessing about it had blown the issue out of all proportion. The difficulty may still exist, but it has become less pressing and all-consuming. It can now be looked at with more distance. Your negative feelings have become less intense. The new perspective allows you to approach the issue more constructively.

WHEN IN DOUBT

Can we discern when in doubt? Can we move forward in life if we leave space for doubt? Our culture wants certainties. Uncertainty and ambiguity must be eliminated immediately. Doubt is synonymous with hesitation and an inability to decide. It is different in Ignatian discernment. There is such a thing as "good doubt"—doubt as a condition and driving force for discernment.

The Good Doubt

Discernment asks that you let go of your certainties and convictions. Listening to your heart requires an interior openness and availability. To discern, it is desirable that you dare not to know. Then it is necessary to leave the various possibilities open. Moreover, you must be prepared to consider unexpected or previously unknown answers. Only those who dare to accept the uncertainty of *not knowing* can fully discern.

> *When he was a young man, life was simple for Jim. He could answer questions immediately. It was yes or no, black or white. Being an adult, he thought, meant making decisions right away. Jim is a little*

Discerning in Particular Situations

older now. Life seems much less simple to him. At the same time, it has become richer and more surprising. He has gained a better understanding of the complexity of life, both in relation to himself and to the world around him. If he is now faced with a slightly more important choice, he no longer makes up his mind right away. He takes the time to consider the different possibilities calmly. The result is sometimes very different from what he had originally imagined. Experience has taught Jim that daring to doubt can improve the quality of his decision.

Doubt as a Driving Force

Doubt, important as it is, is not comfortable. In itself, it is not an ideal. It's good to want to get rid of uncertainty. In a positive way, however, it is doubt that sets the dynamics of discernment in motion and then keeps it going for a while. It is important to choose to remain in doubt and the uncertainty that accompanies it for a sufficiently long period of time. Doubt allows you to shed your own prejudices and certainties. It promotes freer and clearer discernment.

The person who discerns often notices that, after a period, restlessness and uncertainty give way to more peace and confidence. Doubt diminishes or disappears. An answer to the question arises. Discernment requires much concentration and attention. You cannot, however, produce the result yourself. It is given, without you being responsible for it. Discernment is a permanent exercise that consists in humbly giving up control and accepting the need to receive. For the Christian, it is a demanding learning experience to let God alone be at the helm.

TRUST YOUR FEELINGS

WHEN THERE ARE TENSIONS

The word *tension* often has a negative connotation. It evokes a problem that needs to be solved quickly. Without tension, however, no life is possible. Tension in the veins—blood pressure—is a prerequisite for life. Only those who have died have no tension in the body. The same applies to discernment.

People like simple answers. At least they are clear. Opting for a concrete certainty automatically garners more sympathy than accepting complex compromises. Unfortunately, the answers to most of the questions and problems we face are neither black nor white. They lie in the infinite shades of gray. Wisdom lies between the extremes.

> *Liz's environmental awareness means that she won't take a plane, that she uses public transport as much as possible, that she lowers the heating in her house by a few degrees, and so on. But for her work, Liz needs to travel to the other side of the continent from time to time. There are no buses in the village where her grandfather lives. And, because the new baby at home has such fragile lungs, it would be good to put the heating up a little in winter. All this regularly troubles Liz's conscience in a way she cannot easily resolve. She wants to be faithful to her ecological commitment. But she doesn't want to find herself imprisoned by her principles either.*

Many of these tensions are quite normal. They can be uncomfortable and can sometimes be a source of conflict. Often your heart is moved by conflicting feelings that arise from these opposing points of principle. These inner movements of the heart can be seen as invitations. They push you to seek appropriate answers to the concrete questions that life poses through these tensions. Sometimes they also push you to find new solutions to these new problems.

Such tensions force you to be creative and allow you to progress. This is possible only if you allow yourself to be constantly challenged by them. That is better than denying them or trying to make them disappear.

WHEN YOU HAVE DISTURBING THOUGHTS

Temptations are commonplace. They are thoughts, images, memories, or real events that exert a strong attraction. They are difficult to resist because, generally but not always, they can quickly give intense pleasure. The flip side of the coin, however, is that, in the end, temptation is almost always negative.

Ignatius gives three tips on how to deal with temptations and similar disturbing thoughts.

All or Nothing

Charles is happily married. But he has cheated on his wife with Rana. He sincerely regrets it. He really doesn't want to jeopardize his relationship. Flirting has always been his weak point. He has been invited to a party this very evening. He knows Rana will be there. His wife is traveling, so he can go alone. He realizes that if he goes, he's taking a risk. Charles had initially decided not to go, but he has just reread the invitation, and he feels more and more like going anyway.

TRUST YOUR FEELINGS

Ignatius is very clear in the advice he gives in the face of temptations. There is only one effective way to deal with them: shut the door immediately. You must not dialogue with temptation. There is no point in seeking a compromise. You always lose. If you taste even a little bit of the sweet temptation, you are lost. The attraction of temptation quickly becomes so strong that all resistance disappears.

Temptation is in your DNA. It constantly whispers that you are strong enough not to give in and that you can stop immediately. But in the end, the power of seduction is always too great, and it is you who loses out.

If you have spotted a temptation, it is better to turn away immediately and not confront it. Usually, the temptation at this point rapidly loses its power and you can move on to something else. This attitude requires modesty. As a first reaction, you might think that you are strong enough to face the fight and that there is no need to run away from it. But don't do it. Walk away. Afterward, you will feel peace and contentment.

Talking about It

Charles still doesn't know whether to go to this party. His inner tension is palpable. He feels both excitement and fear. He continues to struggle on his own. Charles decides to call his best friend, Martin, although he finds it embarrassing and humiliating. Charles knows that Martin is a wise person and that he likes him. Martin doesn't have to say much. When Charles has explained the situation to him, he simply asks, "And?" The answer becomes immediately obvious to Charles. Tonight, he will go to the cinema with Martin.

Discerning in Particular Situations

Temptations thrive when there is secrecy. It is part of temptation to make you believe, quite convincingly, that it would not be good if you talked to someone about it—it would be humiliating, immature, strange, and not useful.

Ignatius recommends exactly the opposite: to tell a confidant openly what is happening. Immediately, the power of the temptation will diminish, and it will be revealed for what it is—a bad idea.

Accepting Your Weaknesses

Margaret was treated very badly in her youth because of her appearance. As a result, she has little self-confidence, even though she has received excellent therapy. Margaret is now an adult and has built a good life for herself, but if someone at home or at work makes the slightest remark that she interprets as a reference to her appearance, she goes ballistic.

You blame yourself for letting yourself be caught out once again where your defenses are weakest. How is this possible? You know so well where you are vulnerable. Will it never stop? Anger and disappointment at your own stupid behavior can make you doubly unhappy.

Ignatius's advice is as simple as it is obvious. Don't be surprised, upset, disappointed, or angry that you have fallen into the trap once again. This is your weak point. It is obvious that this is where you will be attacked. Maybe one day it will heal. Maybe this vulnerability will fade over the years or you'll learn to manage it better. Maybe you won't.

If you accept it, you will avoid a double pain, and you will be able to live with it more easily.

8

Discernment and Christian Faith

Ignatian discernment gives great importance to positive feelings. Does this mean that it is a subtle way of staying positive and looking at the world artificially through rose-tinted spectacles? No. The foundation of Ignatian discernment is a conviction of faith.

A GOD OF LOVE

Discernment, as Ignatius of Loyola teaches, has a special connection with the Christian faith. The starting point is the belief that God loves every human being. Christians believe that God is a creator God who is committed to everyone. This commitment is not limited to a creation in the distant past. It also applies to today—here and now. Creation means that the Creator lets humankind continually share what he is: life and love. The deepest core of a human being, according to Christians, is this love. The more a person is open to the Spirit of God, the more he or she can experience this love. Joy, hope, and faith, on the one hand, and emptiness, irritation, or anger, on the other, are usually signs of a greater or lesser closeness to God. Discernment is ultimately nothing more than constantly directing your inner antennae toward the Spirit of God. Consequently, a person can discover where the path of life with God is leading them.

Is Joy Always Possible?

Pope Francis, a Jesuit and specialist in Ignatian discernment, once tweeted: *In the heart of the Christian there is joy. Always!*[1] Does this mean that if on a good day you do not feel joyful at all, you're doing something wrong? Of course not. Everyone has their off days. Sometimes, there are more off days than you would like. The same probably goes for Pope Francis. His tweet is not an accusing little finger that says: *Ah well, you call yourself a Christian and you feel angry, annoyed, or sad. This is not right! Aren't you ashamed?* Rather, his tweet expresses hopeful faith in the unceasing presence of God's love in the depths of a person's soul. The art and the challenge of discernment consists in entering and remaining in contact with this deep interiority, which is divine.

Thérèse of Lisieux

Experience shows that this is indeed possible, even in cases of great pain or extreme suffering. Discernment does not take away this pain and suffering. Connection with your

---

1. Pope Francis (@Pontifex), "In the heart of the Christian...," Twitter, February 24, 2017.

inner self can, however, at the same time, bring joy and peace. It is not surprising that Christians call the book of their faith the Good News.

An impressive example is that of Thérèse of Lisieux (1873–1897). Thérèse was a French nun who, at the age of just twenty-four, was slowly suffocated by pulmonary tuberculosis. She wrote the story of her life while on her sickbed. This young woman knew that she would soon die. She was in great physical pain. To make matters worse, she felt little joy in her prayer during the last months of her life. Thérèse, however, was so trained in discernment that, even in these extreme circumstances, she could remain connected to her deepest core, to God himself. Her autobiography is a long song of thanksgiving for all the good that God gave her, even in this last and most difficult stage of her life.

Thérèse's testimony—and that of many others—is so impressive that it may seem beyond reach. Above all, however, it is encouraging and hopeful. It shows how discernment can be refined and how far it can go, even in extreme circumstances. Some are certainly more skilled at it than others. But here, too, the saying that practice makes perfect applies.

Not Only for Christians

Discernment is not only for Christians. The Spirit of God does not allow himself to be enclosed in a single faith or church. Christians believe that the Spirit of God wants to be present and active in every person of good will. This also applies to people who adhere to a different religion or philosophy of life. Nevertheless, Christians have an advantage. Their faith relationship with Jesus Christ, the greatest teacher of love of all time, can particularly prime their hearts to be open to this divine joy.

For non-Christians, the same condition applies, so that their discernment is sufficiently refined and reliable. They must also ensure that their hearts are formed and nurtured within the framework of their own tradition.

9
Community Discernment

Discernment as described in this book is usually at a personal level. It is about a person listening to their inner experience to find clues for their own actions.

Discernment can also take place at the level of a team, a community, a couple, etcetera. Here, too, the question of what is both important and desirable can be asked. Here, too, you can try to discover God's desire through discernment. Community discernment can be a valuable tool for making a choice or for setting priorities for the future together. A process of communal discernment can also make sense as a dynamic of deepening.

> *Some young families live in the same neighborhood. They are all involved as volunteers in the welcoming of refugees. They have been doing this for several years now and notice how important it has become in their lives. They are beginning a process of community discernment to reach a better understanding*

> *of what really motivates them. They will also discern on the question of what form this commitment should take in the years to come.*
>
> *A monastic community has decreased considerably in members over the last few decades. This means that the buildings are now too large. There are also too many different activities. Moreover, the question arises whether new activities should be launched instead of continuing to do what has always been done.*

Personal discernment can be complicated. This is especially true of community discernment. Special care should therefore be taken to formulate clearly and precisely the question that you want to discern, because it is important that all participants can identify sufficiently with the question. Appropriate instruments are also needed to enable community discernment to develop its own dynamics. This is more than the sum of the personal discernment of the individual participants.

CONTEMPLATIVE DIALOGUE

Contemplative dialogue is at the heart of community discernment. It is a special way of sharing and listening in a group, often in an atmosphere of prayer. Contemplative dialogue is characterized by the absence of judgement, respect for the personal feelings and opinions of each person and the nonreactive nature of personal input. Concretely, this means that each participant is given the opportunity to express their personal discernment. Others listen without reacting. In this way, each participant's personal discernment is given a place in the personal discernment of others. Thanks to the succession of contemplative dialogues, a dynamic of community discernment can be created.

ACCOMPANIMENT

Community discernment requires appropriate accompaniment, preferably by a team of external experts. They supervise the process and essentially help to identify common lines or patterns that develop in the group through contemplative dialogues.

COMMON REVIEW

Community discernment does not always have to be aimed at reaching a decision. You can also simply review together a particular period or experience in the way of discernment. If this happens, lessons can be learned from it.

> *Paul and Rose take a few hours every two months to take stock together of their relationship and their family. They combine silence, writing, and conversation. In this way, they try to clarify what is going well, what is more difficult, and what they can learn from it. By mutual agreement, Paul and Rose avoid any discussion during this joint review. They listen to each other. They are regularly surprised by what comes out of it. Now that their children are growing up, Paul and Rose have decided to involve them once a year.*

10
Discernment as a Way of Life

Ignatius learned better than anyone else to use his praying heart as a compass. Discernment became second nature to him. He ended each hour of the day with two minutes of review. In doing this, he developed a unique ability to spot the slightest movement in his heart in real time. He often drew immediate conclusions.

CONTEMPLATIVE IN ACTION

Soon the Jesuits began to describe this way of living as *contemplative in action*. This means that you live in a way that is so connected with your inner self that you can let yourself be guided by what your heart is saying amid the hustle and bustle of daily life. For Christians, contemplation refers to the contemplation of God. Discerning in your daily life, following the example of Ignatius, enables you to become increasingly sensitive to the presence or absence of God and to allow yourself to be guided by him. It is the fruit of a long learning process that requires continuous attention.

GOD IN ALL THINGS

As superior general of the Jesuits, Ignatius of Loyola had to deal with a wide range of issues on an ongoing basis. Some issues were of a spiritual nature, but others were purely material or related to politics in the broadest sense. It was always the subtle art of discernment that showed him the way. The life-giving Spirit of God not only blows within the walls of churches but can be discerned in all the things of life.

> *John is a teacher. His familiarity with the Ignatian review enables him to sense quickly how the children are doing. This often determines the way he approaches them. John has just noticed that Kevin is having difficulties. Instead of doing his sums, the child is constantly looking out the window. John knows that Kevin has a difficult family situation. Rather than reprimanding Kevin, he gives him a pat on the back and a warm smile. During recess, John takes the boy aside and lets him tell his story. When he then has the children do a dictation after the break, Kevin is very attentive and focused.*

We have seen above how discernment can help in making choices and dealing with various situations. Even when nothing special is happening, discernment can help in the ongoing search for a good life. Inner feelings are, to a large extent, things that happen in spite of yourself. To a certain extent, however, you can also deal with your feelings consciously.

Discernment as a Way of Life

Ignatius teaches how a form of conscious spiritual discipline can help you become a happier person.

You can choose to be completely open to certain feelings. You can also choose to return to them later to deepen them. We have seen that this can be especially good for positive and lasting feelings.[2] These experiences can therefore doubly strengthen and nourish you. Conversely, you may decide to limit the impact of negative feelings, as far as possible, and not get swept away by them. In this way, you can avoid them exhausting you unnecessarily.

> *Natalie loves Peter very much. They have been married for over thirty years. Her relationship with her mother-in-law, however, is rather bad. Theresa has never forgiven Natalie for "stealing" her only son. As Theresa gets older, the aggression increases. In the past, Natalie could be devastated by such an "attack" for several days. Sometimes, she wondered whether she could stay with Peter. Over the years, Natalie has learned to manage this situation. She realizes that Peter cannot help her. He has never been able to stand up to his mother. If Theresa attacks her now, it still hurts. But Natalie makes sure that her mother-in-law's rudeness doesn't take too much of her attention. She separates out these painful moments from the rest of her life so that she can live her own life with Peter.*

To this day, countless people around the world benefit from Ignatius of Loyola's expertise. Discernment is not a technique or a method, nor is it a magic trick that you can pull out of your sleeve. It is a way of life. In the twenty-first century, too, you can master it. Discernment is a gift. It is also a choice.

---

2   See section, "Emotional interiority," page 31.

Discernment is not reserved for the privileged few. It can be learned.

ACTIVE *AND* PASSIVE

This book explains what it takes to discern: inner life and sensitivity of the heart, technique, spiritual discipline, awareness of what is going on around you, sharp intellectual analysis, patience, and perseverance.

Discernment asks that you do as much as you can. At the same time, it invites you to let go radically to be able to receive. Discernment is both active and passive. It requires trust and makes trust grow. We discover, again and again, that the answer is given. Your own commitment is necessary. But you don't need to invent an answer or make it up yourself. In the end, discernment is something that happens to you. Discernment requires you to listen to the voice that speaks within your heart. Christians believe that this voice is the voice of God. It points out to each one of us, to everyone, the path of life.

Afterword

This book is the fruit of decades of study, formation, and personal experience in Ignatian discernment as presented in the *Spiritual Exercises* of Ignatius of Loyola. It is not a scholarly book but rather a practical guide, illustrated with many examples. Reading this book does not presuppose any prior knowledge of Ignatian spirituality.

I have therefore chosen to avoid all jargon. The reader will look in vain for technical words such as consolation, desolation, good spirit, evil spirit, enemy of human nature, sin, humility, and the like. It is true that this jargon makes it possible to express precise nuances and subtleties that ordinary language does not offer. Experience has taught me, however, that it often leads to confusion and misunderstanding among the uninitiated. Instead, I use expressions such as emotional foundations, inner life, positive and negative feelings, confrontation, receptivity, and so on. They are not used as such by Ignatius of Loyola, but they seem to me to be more in tune with contemporary language and culture and therefore more appropriate.

Many thanks to Jos Moons, SJ, and Mark Rotsaert, SJ, for their critical reading of the manuscript and their valuable comments. Thanks also to Stephen Noon, SJ, for his careful reading of the English version of the text.

Helpful Links

On Discernment: https://www.ignatianspirituality.com/what-is-ignatian-spirituality/the-ignatian-way/what-is-discernment/.

The Life of Ignatius: www.jesuits.org/stories/the-life-of-st-ignatius-of-loyola/.

SEEL (The Spiritual Exercises in Daily Life) is a Jesuit-organized program of meditations that can be done at home. See www.manresa.ie/ignatian-spirituality/exercises-in-daily-life.

Jesuit Centre of Spirituality, Manresa, Dublin: www.manresa.ie/.

Ignatian Retreat Centers in the United States: https://www.jesuits.org/our-work/retreat-centers/.

Jesuit Spirituality Centers in Canada: https://jesuits.ca/our-work/spiritual-life/.